More
Knowledge

More
Knowledge

More of your
football questions answered

Edited by
James Dart

guardianbooks

Published by Guardian Books 2010

2 4 6 8 10 9 7 5 3 1

First published in Great Britain in 2010 by
Guardian Books
Kings Place, 90 York Way
London N1 9GU

www.guardianbooks.co.uk

A CIP catalogue record for this book
is available from the British Library

ISBN 978-0-85265-147-6

Designed and set by www.carrstudio.co.uk
Printed in Great Britain by CPI Bookmarque Ltd,
Croydon, Surrey

Introduction

More than a decade of fielding your questions and still you want answers. Therein lies the beauty of our weekly Knowledge football column: the desire for information and statistics, the need for sated, enquiring minds. Your queries, quibbles and general trivia-based ramblings arrive in our inbox from around the world, and we don our nerd caps – OK, slightly adjust them – and scour through books, magazines, archives (both dusty and electronic) and websites, as well as employing the odd bit of proper journalistic practice too. Then, if we fail to uncover the answers, reach a dead end in our search for the truth, you, the audience, step in.

In the ten years that the column has been published, we have sought to establish and maintain a quirky, yet original tone and deal with the footballing questions that haven't been asked – and answered – a billion times before. When have a dog and a seagull found the scoresheet? Did a player provoke his team-mate to attack him by breaking wind? Was Steve Ogrizovic arrested on spying charges in Kazakhstan? And is Paolo Maldini really the greatest runner-up in history? In an age when interesting stories in football are on the wane and the game often pales into a bland impersonation of its former self, the Knowledge cares enough to take the road less travelled and answer these questions. It is the dedication and nerdish passion of our writers and readers that enables us to keep bringing you the fascinating, offbeat facts and stories so rarely reported on the modern football pages.

What follows is the second compilation of our favourite questions from readers and the answers faithfully provided by guardian.co.uk's football-writing team since the column began at the turn of the millennium. From the time Niall Quinn rescued easyJet Flight 576 to Newcastle, to the replica Shrewsbury Town shirt that starred in Spinal Tap, this book collates some of the weird, wonderful and, more often than not, downright bizarre facts about the game.

If you have a cunning or inane question to ask about the world of football, that's been bugging you for as long as you can remember, or if you have an answer to a poser that has gone unanswered, drop our crack team of sleuths at knowledge@guardian.co.uk a line. And if you want to lose yourself in the online nerdvana of our archives, be sure to visit the guardian.co.uk/football/series/theknowledge page. In the meantime, I hope you enjoy the selection that follows.

More
Knowledge

"Chippenham Town striker David Pratt was sent off just three seconds into a game against Bashley in 2008. Does that qualify as the fastest sending-off ever?"

Ludicrously, it doesn't. Pratt appeared to have set a new record when he was dismissed for living up to his name and ploughing into Bashley's Chris Knowles after just three seconds of the Bluebirds' 2-1 British Gas Business Premier defeat on 27 December. "You normally won't meet a milder man, but David lost it," admitted the Chippenham secretary George McCaffrey.

But even that effort pales in comparison to the Cross Farm Park Celtic striker Lee Todd. Whereas Pratt received his marching orders for a reckless challenge, Todd got his for foul language at the start of Cross Farm's Sunday league game against Taunton East Reach Wanderers. With his back to the referee Pete Kearle, Todd was startled by the force with which the referee blew his whistle for kick-off. "Fuck me, that was loud," muttered Todd under his breath, but the official heard and promptly produced a red card. "I wasn't swearing at the ref or anyone else," protested Todd afterwards. "He nearly blew my ear off." Not much good it did him: despite appealing to the Football Association, Todd was fined the grand sum of £27 and banned from playing for 35 days. The 10 men of Cross Farm Park Celtic, meanwhile, went on to win the game 11-2.

Other swift sending-offs of note include that of Bologna's Giuseppe Lorenzo, dismissed after 10 seconds for thumping a Parma player, plus the substitutes who saw red without even setting foot on the field of play. During a game for Swansea against Darlington in November 1999, Walter Boyd came on as a replacement seven minutes from time after the Swans had been awarded a free-kick. Before the set piece could be taken, however, the Jamaican became involved in some argy-bargy with opponent Martin Gray; moments later, Gray was on the floor, clutching his head. Referee Clive Wilkes missed the incident, but upon consultation with his assistant, dismissed the striker. "This will go in the record books as nought seconds as the match had not been restarted," the FA statistician Ray Spiller told the Sun. A decade earlier in December 1989, Barnsley's Ian Banks didn't even make it on to the pitch before being given his early bath; he was sent off while warming up to come on as a substitute.

"What is the worst penalty shoot-out in the history of football?"

The penalty kicks in the 1986 European Cup final take some beating, coming as they did in the wake of 120 of the most tedious minutes of football ever witnessed in a major final. Barcelona and Steaua Bucharest were rewarded therefore with a 12-yard shoot-out, at which point both teams missed their first two. The Romanian champions then found their shooting boots and knocked home their next two, but Barça, then managed by Terry Venables, twice more failed to beat Helmuth Ducadam in the Steaua goal. Ducadam, who became known as "the hero of Seville", had saved all four spot-kicks from José Alexanko, Ángel Pedraza, Pichi Alonso and Marcos Alonso, enabling Steaua to run out 2-0 winners.

More worthy of note is Thailand's 1-0 win on penalties against Bangladesh in the 1973 Merdeka tournament, in which Singapore also stuttered to a 1-0 shoot-out victory over Cambodia. But the world record for the worst-ever series of penalty kicks, however, is quite predictably held by a pair of English teams. In January 1998, Under-10 sides Mickleover Lightning Blue Sox and Chellaston Boys B faced off for the Derby Community Cup. The game finished 1-1, but the not-so-sudden-death shoot-out ended up taking longer than the original one-hour game; 62 penalties were missed before Chellaston's Richard Smith broke the deadlock. John Blatherwick remained strong amid the pressure to level from the subsequent kick and when Chellaston missed the 65th attempt, Sam Gadsby mercifully stepped up to score the winner.

"Has a player ever been significantly injured while celebrating a goal?"

Schadenfreude is alive and well in the beautiful game, especially when it comes to needlessly extravagant post-goal jubilations. Take Celestine Babayaro, for instance, who broke his leg when celebrating a pre-season Chelsea goal – against Stevenage – with a misguided somersault, or Lomana LuaLua, who twisted his ankle after landing awkwardly from a backward tumble of his own, having scored for Portsmouth at Arsenal. "He's a one-off," admitted the Pompey boss, Harry Redknapp, with a rueful smile.

The rise and rise of excessive knee-slide celebrations accounted for an embarrassing injury to the Arsenal captain, Patrick Vieira. Possibly attempting to emulate the regular sight of Thierry Henry effortlessly gliding along the pitch on his knees post-goal, Vieira engaged in a rather uncharacteristic version after scoring for the Gunners in a 3-2 win against Manchester United in November 1997. Cue a quad muscle injury that ruled the Frenchman out of action for five weeks and so haunted his manager that Arsène Wenger repeatedly warned striker Emmanuel Adebayor against the celebration in 2008.

Arsenal have form when it comes to self-induced goal glee injuries, mind. Striker Perry Groves once knocked himself unconscious on the roof of the Gunners' dug-out when leaping up to celebrate a goal (luckily for him the physio was sat next to him), while Steve Morrow's name was made for all the wrong reasons when team-mate Tony Adams dropped him to the floor while celebrating the team's 1993 League Cup final triumph over Sheffield Wednesday. "Tony was devastated, but I wasn't angry, it was a complete accident," said the unlucky Morrow, who collected a broken collarbone to go with his winners' medal.

So happy was the Manchester City forward, Shaun Goater, after his team-mate Nicolas Anelka scored at

Birmingham in October 2002 that he booted an advertising hoarding in delight. "I have been getting a bit of stick from the gaffer and the physio and I will not be celebrating in that fashion ever again," admitted a sheepish Goater. Equally unfortunate was Villarreal's Argentinian forward Martin Palermo after he scored in extra-time for Villarreal against Levante in the 2001 Copa del Rey, when a concrete wall collapsed on him as he rushed over to share his joy with the club's supporters. Palermo broke his ankle and was sidelined for six months, while Levante went on to win the game on penalties.

Yet the dubious honour of the most ill-fated goal celebration in history must surely go to the Servette midfielder Paulo Diogo, for whom the fickle finger of fate pointed in a particularly painful direction in a December 2004 Swiss Super League game. After setting up team-mate Jean Beauséjour to score their third goal in a 4-1 away win over Schaffhausen, Diogo wheeled away towards the visiting fans and leapt on to a pitchside fence. Having only recently married, Diogo managed to trap his wedding ring in the barrier, before jumping off; alas, neither the top half of his finger nor his ring came down with him. While frantic stewards searched for the missing digit, unsympathetic referee Florian Etter booked Diogo for excessively celebrating, before his night went from bad to worse in a Zurich hospital when doctors had to amputate what remained of the finger. "When I jumped down from the fence, I didn't feel anything at all," Diogo told Blick later that week. "The first time I noticed that something was missing from my hand was when it started to hurt. And it hurt tremendously." He added philosophically: "I'm not dead and life goes on. So I have to live with one less finger."

"I heard that Diego Maradona once had a trial with Ipswich Town and, for some reason, gave credence to this story. Does anyone have more details?"

Right player, wrong club, we're afraid to say. Diego Maradona actually came closest to signing for Sheffield United, for whom the Argentinian would have played in the late 1970s had it not been for the stinginess of the Blades' board. In 1978, the United manager Harry Haslam watched the 17-year-old Maradona in action on a scouting trip to Argentina and was so impressed he immediately arranged a £200,000 deal. But the transfer fell through when the Second Division club failed to stump up extra cash on top of the fee, so Haslam instead signed Maradona's countryman, the River Plate midfielder Alex Sabella, for £160,000. Sadly, although Sabella wowed the Bramall Lane crowds, he could not prevent the Blades sliding into the Third Division in 1978-79. Sabella was offloaded to Leeds United for £400,000 in 1980 and Sheffield slipped quietly into the Fourth Division later that season. Meanwhile, Diego ...

In mitigation for Ipswich supporters, a few other famous names have trialled and failed at Portman Road, including Ruud Gullit, John Barnes and Paul Gascoigne. Elsewhere, Newcastle could have saved themselves an awful lot of time, money (£15m) and lack of success had they not placed Alan Shearer in goal during a trial, before rejecting him and sending the striker on his merry way to Southampton. Both West Ham and Liverpool passed up on a 15-year-old Kenny Dalglish before he went on to play for Celtic and, er, Liverpool. And the Germany striker Carsten Jancker was sent home from a trial at Luton Town as a youngster, after failing to make a lasting impression upon manager David Pleat. "I really wanted to make it in England," he told the Observer, "but Luton gave me only one game before saying goodbye. And they weren't even in the Premier League."

History could also have been wildly different for St Mirren, had their audacious 2001 move for Ronaldinho not foundered at the final hurdle. The Brazilian had just agreed a £6m switch from Gremio to Paris Saint-Germain, when it was decided by his advisers that he would find a short-term deal elsewhere in Europe to acclimatise before his switch to the city by the Seine. Upon discovering this fact, quick-witted club officials at Love Street made their move, only to be scuppered by red tape as they failed to secure international clearance on a deal. "We spoke to Ronaldinho but there was a legal problem at [Gremio]," claimed the Saints' boss Tom Hendrie. "He was willing to come and play for us before going on to PSG." However, when questioned about this prior to Barcelona's 2008 friendly at Dundee United, Ronaldinho replied: "I had a lot of offers from Europe. I can't remember where they were all from."

"Having watched a parachutist land on the roof of a stand at Turf Moor rather than the pitch, are there any other examples of pre-match 'entertainment' going wrong?"

First up, more on the dunderhead daredevil at Burnley. In August 2008, a member of the "elite" Red Devils parachute team forced the Clarets' Championship game against Ipswich to be delayed by more than an hour after landing on the ground's David Fishwick Stand and then needing to be rescued by the emergency services. "The Red Devils have accepted responsibility and informed the club that the incident was down to individual error," read a club statement. Adding that the incident had caused "major embarrassment" to the club, Burnley went on to suspend all pre-match entertainment at Turf Moor.

This isn't the only instance of a sky-diver missing his target at a football ground. In December 1998, Flight Sergeant Nigel Rogoff parachuted into a blustery pre-game nightmare at Villa Park in a festive Father Christmas attire. Part of a seven-man team, Rogoff came in first but could only hit the roof of the Trinity Road Stand. Supporters could only watch in horror as his parachute proceeded to drag him off the roof and send the helpless

Rogoff falling to the pitch side track. As the remaining six members of the aerial unit managed to land safely, Rogoff was fighting for his life. Amazingly he managed to survive the fall, but suffered severe internal injuries, smashed his pelvis, shattered both hips, broke several ribs and tragically had to have a leg amputated. The story, though, does have a happy ending. During his recovery, Rogoff fell in love with Sarah Collins, one of the nurses at the Defence Services Rehabilitation Centre in Epsom, and the pair later married and had twins. "I may have lost a leg and been forced to give up the career I loved, but it led me to Sarah," said Rogoff.

Also lucky to survive a sickening accident prior to a match was the Wolverhampton Wanderers supporter Denise Butler. Wolves had planned to warm up their crowd prior to a November 2003 game against Newcastle with a fireworks display. Unfortunately, a stray "comet star pyrotechnic effect", as the Jubilee Fireworks managing director Chris Pearce described it, went off horizontally instead of vertically, catching the unlucky Butler full in the face. Seven other fans in the Billy Wright Stand also needed medical treatment. After undergoing surgery to clean and stitch the facial laceration at New Cross hospital, Butler spent two nights there under observation before being discharged. "I can say without doubt now that there will be no more displays here at Molineux," apologised the Wolves chief executive Jez Moxey afterwards.

"I cannot recall a professional player ever having to leave the field due to a call of nature. I am sure this must have happened – has it?"

Such instances, as uneasy on the eye as they may be, certainly have occurred. In December 2009, the Stuttgart goalkeeper Jens Lehmann was caught short during the Champions League win over Unirea Urziceni; the former Arsenal player coolly jumped over advertising hoardings mid-game and relieved himself, only to be interrupted by an Unirea counter-attack. Fortunately for Lehmann, referee Viktor Kassai missed the incident and was therefore unable to book him for leaving the pitch without permission. "I thought he handled it very expertly," declared Horst Heldt, Stuttgart's director of sport. "It was a tricky situation. He could hardly run into the dressing room while play was going on. It reminded me of the Tour de France – sometimes there are simply no options."

DaMarcus Beasley was caught furtively urinating next to the bench while waiting to come on for the United States against Mexico at the 2002 World Cup, while a referee in Qatar also couldn't wait during the September 2009 league match between Al Gharafah and Al Khor and was spotted on camera taking a sneaky leak. As for Sergio Goycochea, the brazen Argentina goalkeeper did not care if he was seen, when he would superstitiously urinate on the pitch before facing a penalty. "It was my lucky charm and I went before every shoot-out," he pronounced. "I was very subtle. Nobody complained."

Unlike the Anderlecht supporters who, quite rightly, got rather peed off when an Athletic Bilbao supporter literally urinated on them from a great height (from the top tier to the massed away support below) during the February 2010 Europa League clash at San Mamés. Bilbao subsequently identified and suspended the fan's club membership indefinitely.

"Have any footballers ever been honoured for their off-field bravery?"

A host of players have received awards for their heroism, having given their lives in the war effort. Among their number are:

Bernard Vann: After playing for Northampton Town, Burton United and Derby County, Vann left the Football League behind to attend Cambridge University (where the Chanticleer, the Jesus College magazine, described him in 1909 as "a dashing forward, possessing both pace and weight") and then begin a career as a chaplain and teacher. After joining the army at the outbreak of the first world war, Vann swiftly rose up the ranks and won the Military Cross during the Battle of Loos in 1915, in which his brother Albert was killed. He won the Victoria Cross in 1918 after the attack on Bellenglise and Lehaucourt, during which, according to the London Gazette, "he led his battalion with great skill across the Canal du Nord through a very thick fog and heavy fire from field and machine guns ... The success of the day was in no small degree due to the splendid gallantry and fine leadership displayed by this officer, who had on all occasions set the highest example of valour." Unfortunately, Vann's VC was a posthumous one: in October of the same year, he was shot through the heart by a sniper's bullet.

Donald Simpson Bell: The only other English footballer to be awarded the VC, Bell played as an amateur for Crystal Palace and Newcastle United (while following a career in teaching), before turning professional in 1912 with Bradford Park Avenue. In 1916, Bell, found himself at the Battle of the Somme and, in July, stuffed his pockets with grenades and attacked – successfully – an enemy machine-gun post. He was killed attempting to repeat his remarkable attack five days later.

William Angus: "No braver deed was ever done in the history of the British Army," wrote Lt Colonel Gemmill, the commanding officer who witnessed Angus's astonishing rescue of his friend, James Martin at Givenchy in June 1915. The pair had grown up in Carluke, Scotland, where Angus worked as a miner before signing for Celtic, for whom he made a single first-team appearance. Unlike Bell and Vann, Angus survived to receive his Victoria Cross, awarded for braving bombs and machine-gun fire to bring the wounded Martin back from under the nose of a German trench. Angus lost an eye in the rescue, but recovered and returned, along with Martin, to his hometown, where he later became president of Carluke Rovers, before his death in 1959. "Carluke may well be proud of her hero," declared an emotional Martin at Angus's VC homecoming ceremony.

Jimmy Speirs: Scotsman Speirs, who began his career at Rangers and then Clyde, scored the winning goal in Bradford City's 1911 FA Cup final triumph and lifted the trophy as captain. After joining Leeds City in 1912, he enlisted with the Queen's Own Cameron Highlanders in 1915, won the Military Medal for "bravery in the field", before ultimately falling in the Battle of Passchendaele in August 1917.

Walter Tull: One of England's first black footballers (during spells with Tottenham and Northampton Town), Tull rose through the ranks to also become the first black Army officer. He was sent to the Italian Front in May 1917, where he led his men in the Battle of Piave and was commended for his "gallantry and coolness under fire". In 1918, he was transferred to France and killed in the last Battle of the Somme. In 1998, the Walter Tull Memorial Garden was opened next to Northampton's Sixfields Stadium, which includes the following epitaph from author Phil Vasili (who later wrote the book Walter Tull, 1888-1918, Officer, Footballer): "Through his actions, Tull ridiculed the barriers of ignorance that tried to deny negroes/mulattos equality with their contemporaries. His life stands testament to a determination to confront those people and those obstacles that sought to diminish him and the world in which he lived. It reveals a man, though rendered breathless in his prime, whose strong heart still beats loudly."

Tim Coleman: Throughout a career that took him to Nottingham Forest, Woolwich Arsenal, Everton, Sunderland and Fulham, the Kettering-born Coleman could boast a formidable scoring record (approximately 188 in 406 games). He even led the first players' strike, before joining the Footballers' Battalion in 1914 upon the suspension of the game and winning the Military Medal for bravery on the Western Front in the build-up to the Somme. Coleman returned to a quiet life in Kent and died aged 59 in 1940, a life which is profiled in far richer detail in George Myerson's book: Fighting for Football: From Woolwich Arsenal to the Western Front, The Story of Football's First Rebel.

David Glen: One of six Brechin players killed during the first world war, Glen (who also played for Dundee United and Millwall) was awarded the Military Medal for bravery before dying at the Battle of Arras on Easter Monday 1917. George Cummings's 1948 pamphlet, Through the Years with Brechin City, described Glen as "a gentlemanly player, feared by all his opponents for his robust style of play. It was no uncommon feat for him to cycle 20-odd miles into Brechin, don the colours and lead his team to victory."

Leigh Richmond Roose: An eccentric, but brilliant Welsh international goalkeeper who spent time with Everton, Stoke and Sunderland during a much-travelled career, Roose was awarded the Military Medal in 1916 for bravery on the first occasion he saw action. "Private Leigh Roose, who had never visited the trenches before, was in the sap when the flammenwerfer attack began," records the regimental history of the Royal Welsh Fusiliers. "He managed to get back along the trench and, though nearly choked with fumes with his clothes burnt, refused to go to the dressing station. He continued to throw bombs until his arm gave out, and then, joining the covering party, used his rifle with great effect." Roose was killed later that year during the Battle of the Somme. For more details on a truly fascinating man, read Lost In France: The Remarkable Life and Death of Leigh Richmond Roose, Football's First Playboy, by Spencer Vignes.

Bert Trautmann: Before becoming a household name with Manchester City, Trautmann served with the Luftwaffe in the Second World War and fought on the Eastern Front for three years, during which time he won five medals, including an Iron Cross. After being transferred to the Western Front, he was captured and moved to a prisoner-of-war camp in Lancashire, where he would later settle and make his life. In 2004, Trautmann received an honorary OBE for his efforts in promoting Anglo-German associations, saying: "I am glad that I was able to do something for the relations in a difficult time."

The Eighth Battalion of the East Surrey Regiment: Last, but certainly not least, comes this courageous group, who attempted to capture Montauban Ridge from the Prussian Guard at the Somme on 1 July 1916 while dribbling four footballs ahead of them as they did so. According to The Queen's Royal Surrey Regiment official website, "Captain WP Nevill had purchased four footballs for his platoons to kick across No Man's Land 'subject to the proviso that proper formation and distance was not lost thereby'. Cpt Nevill promised a reward to the first platoon to score a 'goal' in enemy trenches. At 7.27am, led by Nevill, 'B' Company climbed out of their trenches and the attack commenced. In the face of murderous fire, and sustaining heavy casualties, they charged across the intervening ground with the footballs bouncing encouragingly before them. The combination of Nevill's initiative and their gallantry proved successful and they gained their objective on the Ridge. Sadly, Nevill was not there to pay the reward. He had been killed just outside the German wire."

Two of the footballs were recovered from the site; one sits in the National Army Museum, the other in the Queen's Regiment Museum. The East Surreys were awarded two Distinguished Service Orders, two Distinguished Conduct Medals and nine Military Medals, and were immortalised by "Touchstone" of the Daily Mail as thus: "On through the hail of slaughter, where gallant comrades fall; Where blood is poured like water, they drive the trickling ball; The fear of death before them is but an empty name; True to the land that bore them the Surreys play the game."

"Can you tell me the name of the first British club to play in the European Cup?"

The groundbreaking team was Hibernian's 1955 vintage, which reached the semi-finals (despite not being reigning domestic champions – their reputation and floodlights helped book their place) predominantly thanks to a forward line known as the Famous Five: Gordon Smith, Bobby Johnstone, Lawrie Reilly, Eddie Turnbull and Willie Ormond. In the first round they beat the German champions Rot-Weiss Essen 5-1 over two legs, before easing past Djurgårdens in the quarter-finals, 4-1 on aggregate. But their run came to an abrupt end in the last four when eventual runners-up, Stade de Reims, triumphed 3-0 over the two games.

The first English side to play in the tournament were Manchester United, with Matt Busby telling the Football League (read Alan Hardaker, its totalitarian secretary) where to stick the pressure that had led to Chelsea opting out of the tournament the year before. In their first attempt, they disposed of Anderlecht 12-0 but, like Hibs before them, their first punt in Europe ended with them bowing out one step from the final, as the unstoppable Real Madrid of Puskás and Di Stefano beat them 5-3. The League (read Hardaker) would have trifling revenge after the tragic Munich air crash, helping to block United from competing in the 1958-59 European Cup after Uefa's goodwill offer of a place.

"What misdemeanours have players got up to at their Christmas parties?"

Before we summon the ghosts of Christmas parties past, let's start with something nice and innocent from the 1960s: a Tottenham food fight. "Bill [Nicholson, the Spurs manager] had sent our trainer Cecil Poynton over to haul us out of the pub," recalled Jimmy Greaves of his first Spurs end-of-year shindig. "I can still remember him coming in now, only to be greeted by a cloud of nuts, fag boxes and sausages on sticks, forcing him to retreat, hands on head, back into the road. It launched a food free-for-all. The youth-team players, desperate to stay on good behaviour, were like sitting ducks."

Better a sitting duck than a standing ashtray. That fate befell the Manchester City youth player Jamie Tandy in 2004 when a refreshed Joey Barton mistook his eyelids for a cinderbox and eased a cigar into his left one. Barton was fined three weeks' wages. "My eyeball was full of burning red ash. I had to dig it out with my hands," explained Tandy, who was also found guilty of misconduct, before launching a legal action against Barton for damages in 2008, which resulted in a pay-out of £65,000 to the former trainee 12 months later. "I tried to jump on Joey. The bouncers chucked me out, but Joey just carried on partying like nothing had happened."

You don't necessarily have to get violent to show what you think of a team-mate, mind. In 1998, Newcastle came up with a novel and in no way offensive take on Christmas party fun. The players were each to be given a present: Dietmar Hamann (he's German, tee hee hee) got a copy of Mein Kampf, while the Italian Alessandro Pistone, perceived as lacking fight, was given a fresh sheep's heart. "I'm sure it was a joke," the defender insisted admirably. "The others had some really funny presents too: Temuri Ketsbaia got a hairbrush and Duncan Ferguson a prison shirt."

Dennis Wise had some fun of his own in 2001, when he apparently gave his Leicester City colleague Robbie Savage a teddy bear that had been impaled on a lady's special electrical tool, before reportedly saying: "Take this, because you're the only prick in a Leicester shirt at the moment." A few well-chosen observations later, they were seemingly going at it. "A mountain has been made out of a molehill," claimed manager Dave Bassett. "There was a bit of mickey taking which was a bit pornographic, but that's the way it is. In these politically correct times no one is allowed to go out and enjoy fancy-dress parties."

Life, of course, was more fun when you could hold a dwarf-tossing contest in a pub, which is exactly what Vinnie Jones arranged for the Chelsea lads in the early 1990s. "When only two dwarfs walked through the door, Vinnie enquired: 'Oi, what's your game? We've paid for three, not two,'" recalled former player Tony Cascarino. "One of the players piped up: 'what about Wisey [Dennis Wise] making up the third one?'"

Nevertheless, mistakes are easily made when you've quaffed so much lager and pink champagne that you can't see beyond your own nose. In 2001, West Ham's Australian defender Hayden Foxe mistook the bar at trendy London nightspot Sugar Reef for the urinal, standing on top of it in front of understandably startled guests and staff and spraying his 15 pints of shame all over it. The entire Hammers party were thrown out of the club, while Foxe was fined two weeks' wages. "We live in a society where anything goes and it's sad," sniffed the West Ham boss Glenn Roeder. "You see all sorts of people in back alleys and streets tiddling up walls and it's not acceptable." "The whole thing got blown right out of proportion," retorted Foxe, who was given a free transfer at the end of the season.

Another West Ham centre-half, Neil Ruddock, got in trouble along with team-mate Trevor Sinclair in 1998: Razor met the rozzers when he was arrested after the Hammers' festive fancy-dress party at Secrets nightclub in Romford. Ruddock was charged with affray and Sinclair with criminal damage after a woman claimed that two men had ripped bits off her Mini. Ruddock was later acquitted due to conflicting evidence; Sinclair was fined £250 and forced to pay £225 compensation.

There's more. There's always more. Three Celtic players – Joos Valgaeren, Johan Mjallby and Bobby Petta – spent some time looking at four cold walls in 2002 following a clash with nightclub bouncers and a photographer during some "low-key" pre-Christmas team-bonding on Tyneside. "It would be fair to say the players were in Newcastle in an effort to avoid attention," said a Celtic spokeswoman. She omitted the word "futile". The Daily Record newspaper got wind of the Bhoys' plans and dispatched photographer Paul Chappells to grab a picture of the "festivities". When some of the players attempted to leave Buffalo Joe's "western fun theme bar" on the Gateshead Quays, a fracas ensued, in which the offending camera was allegedly stolen; the three Celtic players were all detained on suspicion of robbery, before all being bailed the next day. "If there is a Christmas party in the next 10 years we will do it privately from now on," said the Celtic manager Martin O'Neill. "Where there is a group of five or more Celtic players out in Glasgow, we will call it an illegal gathering."

It is not exclusively a British disease, mind. Denmark's Stig Tofting, once of Bolton, was sacked by his club side AGF Aarhus for allegedly chinning four of his team-mates at the club's festive gathering. Well, one of them had ripped his shirt. Bayern Munich, meanwhile, dealt out some cold punishment to goalkeeper Oliver Kahn ... for leaving their party too soon. "Kahn must know he has to set an example to the younger players and at the Christmas party he did not behave well," fumed coach Ottmar Hitzfeld. "The captain can't leave early."

Last, but not least are Liverpool, who have had their fair share of infamous antics. There was the time that a figure in a Ku Klux Klan outfit turned up to their fancy-dress party, with Steve McMahon on the door. "You can't come in like that. John Barnes is in there," said McMahon, in no way implying that the outfit would have been absolutely fine had Barnes not been at the club. "No," responded the KKK man, whipping off the hood. "He's in here." Not all

Liverpool footballers have been blessed with Barnes's sense of humour, however. In 1998, Jamie Carragher's idea of impromptu Christmas party fun involved a Hunchback of Notre Dame costume, a bevy of strippers and some whipped cream. It certainly wasn't the last own-goal of his career and it certainly wasn't the last own-goal to be scored at a Christmas party.

"Rochdale brought in a falcon to deal with their pigeon problem at Spotland. Are they the first football club to employ an animal?"

Plenty of clubs have been utilising the unique skills of our feathered friends and other members of the animal kingdom. And not all in a bid to keep a lid on pigeon guano. Take Bitchy the hawk, for instance, so named after a fans' poll on the Toronto FC website. The club brought in the Harris Hawk in 2007 to help keep their BMO Field clear of pesky seagulls that hopped over from nearby Lake Ontario to enjoy a good meal at the ground. "Her job is pretty simple – it's to sit and watch the game from the highest vantage point possible," said Mike Gilvin, the vice-president of Toronto's Wildlife Management Programs. "Gulls don't want to fly underneath a predatory bird, so by putting her up high we ensure that the gulls don't come in and land on the pitch or disturb the spectators."

It might be an idea for someone to suggest this humane solution to Staines Town, who angered animal rights activists with their more direct methods of pigeon removal in October 2008. An online posting on the club's forum by commercial manager Angie Payne revealed that the club had "solved the problem – a pest control company came in last week and shot 15 of them. They were a bloody nuisance and if I'd had a gun I would have done it myself." Pigeon Welfare Group campaigner Kathy Green responded angrily. "What they have done is totally barbaric and unethical," she said. "Shooting birds is not an effective deterrent."

At least this prevented the unedifying spectacle of a player booting a poor pigeon into the afterlife at a December 2008 game between San Lorenzo and Tigre in Argentina. Feathers flew when the San Lorenzo defender Gastón Aguirre's shot struck a helpless bird. "I kicked the ball and ... poor pigeon. Now I will be remembered as 'the pigeon killer'," said a mortified Aguirre.

Eintracht Frankfurt have employed a golden eagle named Attila as their real-life mascot since 2005 ("he has been a guest in a multitude of TV shows," explains the club's website), while a goat has been the mascot of fellow German club 1. FC Köln since the 1960s when circus owner Carola Williams donated Hennes to the club (their nickname is Die Geißböcke, or "the billy goats"). Hennes VIII is the present incumbent. These days, though, mammals are something of a rarity at football stadia. In years gone by, of course, livestock were often allowed to graze on the pitches; in the 1920s the Ipswich Town groundsman Walter Woollard kept sheep, goats and chickens in a stand at Portman Road.

Hereford United, nicknamed the Bulls, of course, used to parade one of their namesakes around Edgar Street before games, though it's not quite as good a story as this, however. In 1999 FC Zurich's bull mascot, named Maradona, ("bought by fans after it was threatened with an appointment at the local abattoir," according to an AFP report) escaped its minder at the club's Letzigrund stadium prior to their game against St Gallen, chased players warming up for the game, somehow clambered into the stands and proceeded to run about to its heart's content for a good 10 minutes before being rounded up by brave home supporters.

Even a pair of fish have been taken on by a club. In 2005, floods in Cumbria were responsible for the unlikely journeys of Judy and – inevitably – Billy the goldfish, washed from their comfortable tank in a house opposite Carlisle United's Brunton Park to a goalmouth on the pitch, where they were fortuitously rescued by Emma Story, the daughter of club owner Fred. The club won their next game against Redditch and, as Emma pointed out, "fans began to say the fish represented the fighting spirit of the club". The pair took up residence as the club's mascots and can claim to have played their own small role in the club's rise to League One.

Some of football's most unlikely animal employees, however, can be traced back to the formative days of Manchester United, when they were Newton Heath FC. It transpires that United's early years were replete with fun of the four-legged variety, including Major the fund-raising St Bernard and Billy the alcoholic goat, who sadly succumbed to alcohol poisoning amid the club's celebrations following the 1909 FA Cup final. Major, the pet of Newton Heath skipper Harry Stafford, was utilised as a mobile collection box – he had one tied around his neck – at a fund-raising bazaar for the club when times were breadline-tight in 1901. Having not taken too kindly to this hard graft, Major escaped, only to be discovered by a rich local brewer by the name of John Henry Davies, whose daughter became particularly attached to the canine. After locating Stafford and proposing to buy Major, Davies learned of Newton Heath's predicament. Soon after he formed a takeover consortium with Stafford and other businessmen, the group changed the club's name and the rest, as they say, is history.

"Can anyone enlighten me as to how Alan Hansen received the huge scar that figures so prominently on his forehead?"

As a fresh-faced 17-year-old, Hansen and his schoolmates were late for a volleyball game at Denny and he led from the front in the rush to get to the away school's changing-rooms. Albeit neglecting to acknowledge the minor detail of a glass door in front of him. "I was in hospital for four hours," Hansen told the Scotsman. "I was lucky – the scar stopped right at the top of my right eye. I had 27 stitches in my head and my legs were cut to ribbons." He sued the education authority and won.

"There was once an Italian footballer who was badly injured in pre-season and missed the remainder of the campaign, the last season of his contract. When it came to negotiations, he offered to play for the Italian minimum wage for a year, as thanks for the team's faith in him to recover. What was the fellow's name and have there been other acts of selflessness by professional footballers?"

The player in question was Damiano Tommasi and the rather hazy details recalled are largely correct. In 2005, the Roma midfielder did indeed ask to be paid the Italian minimum wage of €1,500 (£1,013 at the time) a month, because of his injury problems, caused, as it happens, by a clumsy tackle by Gerry Taggart during a pre-season game against Stoke City a year earlier. The gesture did not go unnoticed. L'Osservatore Romano, the Vatican's official mouthpiece, even feted Tommasi in its papal editorial, writing that his was an "unusual decision ... in a world where others earn hundreds of thousands of euros and in which those who already earn millions ask excessive amounts to renew their contracts."

Vatican pin-up Tommasi, a practising Catholic and former altar boy, admitted he made the offer "because I love Roma and football". Also heavily involved in charity work, anima candida ("candid soul" as he is nicknamed), Tommasi is known to use his team-mates' disciplinary fines to contribute towards worthy causes, such as the creation of a football centre in Kosovo.

The Sunderland chairman Niall Quinn displayed similar munificence when a player at the Stadium of Light, handing over to charity the £1m-plus in profits generated from his testimonial match in 2002. "It isn't me standing up and deserving credit," he told the Sunday Times, speaking honestly about his career off the pitch. "This is my way of fighting my demons. I have abused the privileged life I have had and if this match is anything, it is me paying my debt." As if to underline his legendary status among Black Cats supporters, Quinn forked out £8,000 from his own pocket to ferry 80 of them from Bristol to Sunderland late on a Saturday night after they forced the cancellation of an easyJet flight in 2007.

Travelling home after a 1-0 win at Cardiff, the supporters' "unacceptable behaviour onboard", as a spokeswoman from the airline put it (they were singing the club favourite refrain Niall Quinn's Disco Pants), resulted in Flight 576 to Newcastle being grounded. According to the Sunderland Echo, Quinn and fellow members of staff "ordered a fleet of 14 taxis and four six-seater minibuses for the trip back to Wearside". Quinn, who disputed easyJet's account of the incident, later reported that "everyone returned home safely and we will now draw a line under this. To any fans who still feel aggrieved, remember the three points came home as well." He was awarded an honorary MBE in 2007.

Newly-rich-beyond-their-wildest-dreams QPR can point to lifelong Hoops fan Lee Cook, as well as Tommasi (who spent a season at Loftus Road in 2007-08). When he moved to Fulham for £2.5m in August 2007, Cook donated £250,000 out of his own pocket to ease the then dire financial situation at the club. "The club were saying that not enough money had been paid for me," explained Cook. "I said, 'I'll give you 10% of the sale'. It was totally my decision – there was no pressure from anyone. The transfer had been agreed but I love Rangers and I don't want to see them hard up." Strapped for cash is the one thing QPR do not have to worry about any more, and the new moneyed owners even re-signed Cook on loan with a view to a permanent move in the summer of 2008 following his injury-ruined season at Craven Cottage.

Another footballing philanthropist was Don Hutchison, who displayed his generosity to Luton Town in the summer of 2008, even after he had left the cash-strapped club. Having refused to accept his final pay packet before leaving Kenilworth Road, Hutchison sponsored two of the Hatters' youth-team players for the 2008-09 campaign. "This is a truly amazing gesture," enthused the Luton managing director, Geoff Sweet. "This shows the type of man that Don is and what football means to him. His generosity is unique in the modern game."

Not quite. The former Hibernian, Reading and Aston Villa defender Ulises de la Cruz would donate around 20% of his salary to fund projects in the Ecuadorian village of his birth, Piquiucho. Projects undertaken by his Fundecruz charity include work on a school and providing housing, fresh water, jobs and medical services for the villagers. "I never forget what my origins are," said de la Cruz during his time in England. "I respect everybody's take on life but I'm frustrated that so many players focus on their next big house or next big car."

Other diamonds in the rough include the former Leeds United and Republic of Ireland right-back Gary Kelly, who took a leaf out of Quinn's book and donated the £500,000 raised from his testimonial to two cancer charities; Mauricio Taricco, who belied his tempestuous on-field persona by offering to rip up his West Ham contract after tearing a hamstring on his debut (the club accepted, humbled manager Alan Pardew admitting: "This is one of the most honest acts I have experienced"); and Internazionale's Argentinian international Javier Zanetti, who, along with his wife Paula, founded Fundación Pupi, an organisation which helps underprivileged children in his homeland.

One of the more surprisingly altruistic players, however, is the man behind the Craig Bellamy Foundation, established in 2008 by the Wales international in the wake of a trip he made to Sierra Leone a year prior. Moved as he was by the deprivation in the civil-war-ravaged country, but equally by their enthusiasm for football, the Premier League in particular, Bellamy began working on the inception of an organisation that would, as its website now states, "establish a nationwide development league and academy with the aim of using football as a vehicle for positive social development". With a reported £650,000 of his money already invested in the project, Bellamy insisted that he would stick with it "until I'm a very old man". He told the Times: "Because of what's happened over the years with the war, children haven't had any opportunity; they haven't been thrown a football, they've been thrown a gun. Now we can give them a chance that their fathers or grandfathers never had. That's the buzz for me."

"Is there any evidence that awarding three points for a win has made the game more exciting? Would any English championships have been decided differently under the old system?"

In 1980-81, the final season that the English league used the old two-point system, there were 118 draws in the First Division. The following year, with the new reward up for grabs, there were 121. What about the 1994-95 Premiership table, the last time in which the same number of games were played? Er, 134 draws.

Whether or not this is more exciting is purely subjective, but changing the points system made no difference to the destination of any titles post-1982. However, in the 1974-75 campaign, three points for a win would have rewritten the history books. That season Derby County finished top with 53 points, ahead of Liverpool and Ipswich on 51. But Ipswich had won 23 games, two more than the Rams and three more than the Reds, and under the three-points-for-a-win structure Bobby Robson's men would have pinched the title on goal difference.

"Kaká has made it pretty clear that he 'belongs to Jesus', but have any other players publicly displayed their religious views on the field?"

Nicknamed Kaká because younger brother Rodrigo could not pronounce his first name, Ricardo Izecson dos Santos Leite is one of the more high-profile figures to display their religious affiliations in front of millions, unveiling the message "I belong to Jesus" on a T-shirt after Brazil's 2002 World Cup triumph and Milan's victory over Liverpool in the 2007 Champions League final. "I thank God for all the victories and conquests I've had this year as a player and I bring to the altar two prizes," he said in 2008. "This is first my son [Luca] who is about to be born. The other is my [world player of the year] trophy from Fifa, which I want to dedicate to God."

The Everton midfielder Steven Pienaar picked up a booking for flaunting a similar message at White Hart Lane in November 2008, removing his Everton top after scoring the game's only goal to show a T-shirt with "God is great" emblazoned across it. And the Brazilian forward Junior, formerly of the Bescot Stadium, would lift up his shirt during the 2002-03 season to reveal a slogan underneath which read "Jesus lives in Walsall". The Son of God must have resided in Derby and Watford as well, because that's where Junior subsequently hot-footed it to.

Bayern Munich's France international Franck Ribéry, meanwhile, is a devoted Muslim, having converted to Islam and adopted the name "Bilal" when he married Wahiba, his French wife of Moroccan descent. "As a kid, I spent all my time with Muslims. It is my choice. No one told me to do it," said Ribéry, who opens up his hands in supplication to Allah before every match. As does Frédéric Kanouté of Sevilla, who attempted to cover the 888.com advertising on his shirt because gambling was against his religion. Kanouté was even booked and fined €3,000 by the Spanish Soccer Federation for celebrating a goal against Deportivo de La Coruña in January 2009 by displaying the word "Palestina" and other Arabic words on a T-shirt beneath his kit. Article 120 of the rules and regulations in Spain prohibits players from displaying religious or political messages on the pitch. "I am calm with my conscience," said Kanouté of his support for Palestine, "and I believe that I did what I had to do."

Less successful in protesting at Israel's bombardment of Gaza at the same time was the Rangers defender Madjid Bougherra. "I want people to know I do not agree with what is happening in Gaza and throughout Palestine," said the Algerian. "All Muslim players must make a gesture." The Scottish Football Association hid behind Fifa's rules forbidding "personal, political or religious slogans" to be worn on kit, and stopped Bougherra staging his black armband protest.

Getting his message across was something devout Christian Marvin Andrews had little trouble in doing while at Ibrox, however. "If it wasn't for God, we wouldn't have won the league," he told the Times after the Gers' memorable league title triumph in 2005 (Scott McDonald scored twice for Motherwell in the final two minutes of the season to deny Celtic). "Because I am a servant, He will never leave me nor forsake me. He did it for me and the team to show the team that He is God, to show that team that what is impossible with men is possible with God." Andrews even spurned an operation on a cruciate ligament injury, choosing prayer over the surgeon's knife. "God told me not to have the operation," he offered by way of an explanation. Reinforcing his religious outlook, Andrews told the Guardian in 2007 why homosexuality "is against the word of God", adding that "the Bible said that it's an abomination to God; that God created a man to be with a woman or a woman to be with a man. Simple as that."

"Who is the most-capped England player never to have taken part in an international at Wembley?"

Bob Crompton is a Blackburn legend first and foremost – the slug-moustachioed defender played 528 games for the club during a 24-year period in the early 1900s, going on to manage the club twice and dying from a heart attack while still in office in 1941 – but he also made his mark on the international scene, collecting 41 England caps between 1902 and 1914. Those 41 appearances, at a time when rarely more than three internationals were played in a calendar year, represent a record: not one of them took place at Wembley, the stadium of course not being constructed until 1923.

Regarding players in the modern era, Danny Mills played 19 times while the new Wembley was being built, while the protracted assembling of the stadium's second form also meant that Sven-Goran Eriksson became the only England manager never to have sent a team out at the famous stadium. Each and every one of his 67 games in charge between 2001 and 2006 were played during Wembley's building-site days.

"After reading about Claudio Taffarel's stint with his local church team, it got me wondering: which other famous players had loaned their skills to part-time football?"

Dee Why, an amateur club based in the north Sydney suburb of the same name, enticed one George Best to play for them during his holiday there in July 1983; in an exhibition match against Manly Warringah, Best inevitably popped up to score the winner. No less unlikely was the legendary September 1999 Dutch amateur league clash in which former Dutch internationals Ruud Gullit and Marco van Basten went head to head. When Gullit got wind that van Basten would be turning out for the ABN-Amro sixth XI, he agreed to a request from his friends in the AFC fifths team to level the playing field. According to a Guardian report at the time, "the game kicked off with Gullit but without his former team-mate, who had fallen asleep on the sofa at home. However, woken by a phone call, van Basten tore to the ground, where he was immediately brought on as a substitute. Eleven seconds later he had scored. He got another later, but Gullit's team won 6-2."

The former Sheffield Wednesday trio Chris Waddle, Nigel Spackman and David Hirst trotted out for Brunsmeer Athletic of the Meadowhall Sheffield & District Sunday Football League, an outfit which produced former youth products Scott Sellars, Kevin Pressman and, er, Uriah Rennie.

Across the Atlantic, meanwhile, Julio César Romero, Roberto Cabañas and other famous Paraguayan forty-somethings, played for Sol de América in the Golden Age League, a competition set up in Queens, New York, for over-40 footballers from Central and South America, who have all emigrated there. "I grew up like everyone in my country, watching these guys playing on television as national heroes," team-mate Miguel González told the New York Times. "It's exciting but it's strange. You have some of the best players in history playing in this park and no one knows it."

Also flying under radar – for a short time, at least – was Jürgen Klinsmann, who turned out for Orange County Blue Star in California, having relocated there in 2003, scoring as many as five goals in eight games, along with three assists (according to some sources), to take his side into the American Premier Development League play-offs. But opposition players were largely unaware they were contending with a World Cup winner: Klinsmann was registered under the pseudonym Jay Göppingen, named after the town of Göppingen where he was born. Eventually rumbled by the press, Klinsmann was asked by USA Today how his game was holding up. "It's slower," he replied.

"Where on earth does Charlton Athletic's 'Addicks' nickname come from?"

According to the club's official website, "the majority of Charlton historians agree the most likely explanation dates back to a fish and chip shop in 1908 and that 'Addicks' derived from 'haddock'. At that time, Arthur Bryan was a local fishmonger who helped underwrite the cost of establishing Charlton at The Valley, and the club and its opposition used to dine on [his] fish suppers following matches. The story goes that if the team lost they would dine on the less popular cod, but a victory would secure a haddock supper."

It appears the club were even called "The Haddocks", as first depicted in a Kentish Independent newspaper cartoon from October 1908, before becoming "The Addicks" by 1910 (although "The Haddicks" was also used), while a potentially fishy legend has it that the club's 1909 Woolwich Cup final win against Army Service Corps prompted Bryan to parade a host of hefty haddocks around the Creed's Farm ground on poles.

"Does any top player have a more impressive collection of runners-up medals than Michael Ballack?"

We should probably start by appraising Ballack's career as a bridesmaid. You might think that 2008 was far out in front in annus horribilis stakes, with the Premier League, Champions League, Carling Cup (all with Chelsea) and the European Championships (with Germany) all providing him with second prizes. However, Ballack had been there before, missing out on the Bundesliga, Champions League, DFB-Ligapokal (all with Bayer Leverkusen) and World Cup in 2002. He also owns three more Bundesliga runners-up medals (two with Leverkusen in 1999 and 2000, plus one with Bayern Munich in 2004) and another Premier League silver with Chelsea from 2007.

That makes a total of 12 rueful pats on the back for Ballack by the dawn of 2010, though we should probably also mention that he's also been a champion on six occasions, too. Given his prowess at losing, however, it is not such a surprise that he misses out on the biggest loser "honour" to boot. The former Celtic and Scotland midfielder, Paul McStay, became used to life at No. 2, having been a member of the Celtic squad that finished second in the SPL on six occasions (1983, 1984, 1985, 1987, 1996 and 1997), lost two Scottish Cup finals (1984 and 1990), plus four Scottish League Cup finals (1984, 1987, 1991 and 1995). This would tie him with Ballack but for the fact that McStay also played in the 1989 Rous

Cup in which Scotland finished second to England.

Scotland can lay claim to a player with even more memories of second-place heartbreaks, though. Sandy Jardine won runners-up medals in the Scottish top-flight on seven occasions (1967, 1968, 1969, 1970, 1973, 1977 and 1979) and in the Scottish Cup three times (1977, 1980 and 1982). And that was just with Rangers. Jardine went on to achieve second-best with Hearts in Scottish Division One (1983) again in the SPL (1986 and 1988), as well as in the 1986 Scottish Cup. To top all that off, he captained the Scotland team that finished as runners-up to England in the 1975 Home Championship, setting the bar at 15.

However, our outstanding contender comes from the continent and may come as a surprise to some. Despite all his successes (24 major honours at our last count), the Milan legend Paolo Maldini has missed out on the cigar a good few times as well: three Champions League final defeats (1993, 1995 and 2005), three in the Intercontinental/World Club Cups (1993, 1994 and 2003), two in the Coppa Italia (1990 and 1998), three in the Supercoppa Italia (1996, 1999 and 2003), one Uefa Super Cup final defeat (1993) and the three times Milan have come up one place short in Serie A (1990, 1991 and 2005). Add those to Italy's World Cup final defeat to Brazil (1994) and their Euro 2000 reverse against France and it is a grand total of 17 near-misses for the veteran Italian.

"Given the current precarious world economic climate, have any clubs taken up a sideline business to stay afloat?"

Life is all well and good in the world of football global branding, especially for the world's leading clubs. But spare a thought for those a little further down the ladder, such as Croatian third division outfit NK Nedeljanec. In 2004, when officials publicly revealed Nedeljanec's financial strife, a plan was hatched by dedicated fans to save their team's skins: the sale of potatoes, six tonnes of which were collected and then sold to raise club funds. "No one here has much money, but we have lots of potatoes to sell," fans' chief Ivan Fosnar told the Jutarnji List newspaper. "It is the least we can do seeing as we are so near to promotion to the second division. We'll do everything we can to help our club. It is not a problem to donate these potatoes if that will be enough to save the club." Grateful Nedeljanec officials had no, ahem, chip on their shoulder and accepted the donation, which they admitted would help the club survive until the end of the season.

"What is the strangest reason for a match to be abandoned?"

In December 2008, referee Philip Simpson called time on the South Yorkshire Sunday League Cup clash between Mosborough and Royston Village when a player who had already been sent off stormed back on to the field alleg-edly tooled up with a golf club and a machete. According to the Sheffield Telegraph, with 10 minutes remaining and Mosborough 3-2 up, the dismissed Royston player "began chasing people on the pitch" before being "restrained by players and officials". "I just stopped the game straight away and got everyone off the pitch to safety," explained Simpson afterwards, while a shocked Mosborough spokes-man added: "It was a great game ruined by an idiot. I feel sorry for Royston because of the consequences it could have." The Sheffield and Hallamshire County FA said it would in-vestigate the incident.

Less serious but a random abandonment all the same was the League of Ireland Division One encounter between Wexford Youths and Limerick 37 in October 2008, prompted by a row over, of all things, pre-match limbering-up. "Limerick refused to warm up on our second pitch and asked to train on the match pitch," claimed the Wexford Youths manager and owner, Mick Wallace. "In our 18-month history in the First Division, no team in the league has warmed up on the match pitch before the game. Limerick have been here five times and warmed up on the second pitch on each occasion." Wallace then hinted at an ulterior motive from the visitors, suggesting that "Limerick did not want to play the game. Two of their better players were not in the starting XI for some reason." Limerick responded by releasing a statement in which the club refuted the allegations, while a separate statement from their squad added that "there was insufficient lighting provided [on the warm-up pitch] and the safety of the players would be put at risk". The league's disciplinary committee was unsatisfied with this explanation and awarded Wexford a 3-0 win, with Limerick fined €1,000 to boot.

At least the Sunday League Two game between Peterborough North End and Royal Mail AYL in January 2005 kicked off, though referee Andy Wain probably wished it had not after sending himself off for an early bath. With 63 minutes on the clock, Wain awarded the posties a dubious goal to put them 2-1 ahead. "North End's goalkeeper, Richard McGaffin, complained, Wain threw down his whistle, pulled his shirt out and eyeballed the player," detailed a report in the Observer. "Then, unbelievably, he sent himself off. The game had to be abandoned and the referee (who had been experiencing personal problems), explained later: 'If a player did that I would send him off – so I had to go'."

A host of infamous mass-red-card incidents have forced the premature termination of matches, the highlight surely coming in the bad-tempered friendly between Scottish football writers and politicians in October 2008. The Labour MSP John Park was given his marching orders for a tackle on the BBC pundit Chick Young, sparking a mass brawl that forced the shocked referee to call a halt to the game. "John Park did me," an incandescent Young told the Daily Record. "I've got six stud marks down my leg. Their [the politicians'] behaviour was a scandal. They were thugs." The Radio Clyde presenter, Peter Martin added on Sky News that Park was "like something out of the film Hellraiser. I turned to one of their guys and said 'he must be a rugby player, because he's booted me, he's almost broken my team-mate's leg and we're just 10 minutes into the game'."

"It was a bit wet, the ball bounced, I tackled Chick and he hurt himself. I apologised. I was not trying to do him," responded Park, a regional list member for Mid Scotland and Fife. "The ball was there. These things happen on every football pitch in Scotland every week." Frank McAveety, Scotland's former sports minister, meanwhile was accused of threatening the journalists and swearing at the referee, claims he steadfastly denied. "I was moral rectitude," he declared. "Perhaps these complaints have something to do with the fact the parliamentarians were winning [6-2 after 55 minutes] and some players went in a huff." However, the Labour MSP captain Ken Macintosh admitted his team's conduct had left a lot to be desired. "Normally it's our football that embarrasses, not our behaviour," he admitted. "But in this case it wasn't a terrific display." Soon after, the MSPs organised another match, this time against a religious team of priests, ministers and rabbis. "If this game doesn't get us back on the straight and narrow, we've also been offered a match against the police," Macintosh deadpanned.

While technically not an abandonment, the November 2008 suspension of Soudley's Gloucestershire North Senior Division Two matches are worthy of a mention. After their Recreation Ground pitch had been returfed – at a cost of almost £1,000 – wild boars broke through a perimeter fence and began digging up the pitch with their snouts. "Usually it's motorbikes or cars that tear up pitches, not boars," admitted the Gloucester FA operations manager, Chris Lucker. It took months to repair the damage of the hooligan hogs.

Perhaps the most unlikely and abrupt ending of all was the Kenyan Premier League match between Nairobi rivals Gor Mahia and Mathare United in August 2008, which was called off at half-time when the referee and his assistants were held at ransom by incensed Gor supporters at what they perceived to be his poor performance. The Daily Nation newspaper reported that "referee Frank Musungu came under heavy criticism from the fans over the way he handled the match, especially when he awarded United a free-kick at the edge of the box, which was struck in by midfielder Austine Makacha in the 35th minute. The fans blocked the officials in the changing rooms, forcing match commissar Robert Anangwe to call off the match with United leading 1-0."

"How close did the Manchester United goalkeeper Edwin van der Sar come to setting a new world record for consecutive clean sheets?"

Not very, is the short answer. Van der Sar's 1,212 minutes without conceding a goal during the period from 6 November 2008 to 14 February 2009 does not even register in history's top 10 goalkeeping shut-outs. The Fifaapproved International Federation of Football History and Statistics lists the mean keepers as follows:

1. Geraldo Pereira de Matos Filho (Vasco da Gama, Brazil) 1,816 minutes 2. Thabet El-Batal (National, Egypt) 1,442 minutes 3. Dany Verlinden (Club Brugge, Belgium) 1,390 minutes 4. José María Buljubasich (Universidad Católica Santiago, Argentina) 1,352 minutes 5. Thabet El-Batal (National, Egypt) 1,325 minutes 6. Essam El-Hadari (National, Egypt) 1,288 minutes 7. Abel Resino (Atlético Madrid, Spain) 1,275 minutes 8. Gaëtan Huard (Bordeaux, France) 1,266 minutes 9. Zetti (Palmeiras, Brazil) 1,242 minutes 10. Marios Praxitelous (Omonia Nicosia, Cyprus) 1,221 minutes.

There remains some doubt over the legitimacy of the record holder (who was otherwise known as Mazarópi), with several of the 20-and-a-bit matches he kept clean sheets in played at a regional level. But if his mark, registered between 18 May 1977 and 7 September 1978, is good enough for the IFFHS it is good enough for us.

"Has any country completed the significant double of being European champions and Eurovision winners?"

Only three nations are lucky enough to have held both awards at the same time. Spain were the first, winning the European Championship in 1964 with a 2-1 win over the Soviet Union and following it up with a Eurovision win in April 1968 at the Royal Albert Hall, when La La La by Massiel controversially pipped Cliff Richards's Congratulations by a solitary point (the Spanish documentary maker, Montse Fernandez Vila, alleged in her 2008 film, "1968. I lived through the Spanish May", that Franco's fascist regime had bought votes to rig the contest). It was not until June that Italy won the 1968 European Championship final to end Spain's dual reign.

The second country is – surprise, surprise – Germany, or to be more precise, West Germany. They won the Euros in 1980 with a 2-1 win against Belgium, and two years later notched up the double when the unforgettable Nicole led them to Eurovision glory with Ein Bißchen Frieden (A Little Peace). Interestingly, that year the contest was held at the Conference Centre in Harrogate and was presented by Jan Leeming.

And in 2005 Greece followed up their unexpected Euro 2004 triumph when Helena Paparizou's My Number One beat Malta into second place in Kyiv to spark another party to remember on the streets of Athens. The song also claimed a Eurovision record, tallying an average score of just 6.05 points per jury.

"Which was the first professional football club to play under floodlights?"

Portsmouth staged the inaugural floodlit Football League match in February 1956, when 15,831 fans turned up at

Fratton Park to watch Newcastle win 2-0 in Division One, although this was well down on Pompey's regular 21,000 home gate that season. "The public did have concerns that, under lights, not only would fans not be able to see all four corners of the pitch, but the referees and linesmen wouldn't either," Richard Owen, the club's historian, told The Times. Even then the game was almost called off when electricians were called into action after a power failure. "Unkind critics may say that it was a pity that the lights were ever put on," read the Portsmouth Evening News's report.

Matches had been illuminated since the FA lifted its ban on them in 1951, though it was not until September 1955 that Kidderminster Harriers and Brierley Hill Alliance met in the first competitive game to be played under floodlights in an FA Cup preliminary round replay. Arguably the most famous matches to be staged at night, though, were English champions Wolves's 1954 midweek friendlies against the best club teams in the world. After beating Celtic, Racing Club, Moscow Dynamo and Spartak Moscow (Austria Vienna held them to a goalless draw), Wolves arranged a game against the Magical Magyar-laden Hungarian giants Honved. Wearing satin shirts that the club believed would stand out better under the lights, Wolves fought back from 2-0 down to triumph 3-2 and send the nation's press into an all too recognisable frenzy, the next morning's Daily Mail headline excitably bugling: "Wolves champions of the world now."

The idea of glamour evening friendlies had already been visited by the Arsenal manager Herbert Chapman, whose two-decade-long crusade to bring floodlit football to the English finally became a reality in September 1951, when Hapoel Tel Aviv were thrashed 6-1 at Highbury. "Now that I have seen more of soccer by floodlight, I am convinced it will be the means of saving the game from serious decline," wrote the previously sceptical Charles Buchan in a 1951 edition of his Football Monthly. "There are already signs in falling attendances in league games that the post-war boom is over and that something new is required to keep the enthusiasm of the public at its present height."

Headington United (now Oxford United) can pre-date this after installing lights for a friendly against local team Banbury Spencer in December 1950, while non-league South Liverpool had already installed floodlights on telegraph poles at their Holly Park Ground in September 1949. But the first match in England under lights took place between the Sheffield FA-selected teams, the Reds and the Blues, at Bramall Lane on 14 October 1878. As Jon Henderson recalled in the Observer, this "was the first attempt to establish the public's appetite for watching sport after factories closed for the day. Four sets of lights, powered by Siemens dynamos and each emitting 8,000 candlepower, were rigged up on wooden towers. The organisers proved their point when a crowd estimated at 20,000 – 6,000 of whom slipped in under cover of darkness – turned up, which was considerably more than attended that year's FA Cup final."

"Who holds the record for the fastest ever hat-trick?"

Robbie Fowler famously beat the Arsenal keeper David Seaman three times in 273 seconds for Liverpool in August 1994, which remains a Premier League record, although Nigel Clough's treble in four minutes flat for Nottingham Forest against QPR in December 1987 holds the English top-flight record.

The quickest Football League hat-trick took just 140 seconds to compile and was the rather swift work of James Hayter. Coming off the bench in the 84th minute, the Bournemouth forward wasted little time as he scored three times in a 6-0 win over shell-shocked Wrexham in February 2004. "I did not think I would get on, so to come on and score three goals is unbelievable," admitted Hayter, whose parents and brother missed the achievement by leaving the game early to beat the rush of fans and get a ferry home to the Isle of Wight. "It's not easy to get over from there. I fully understand why they left early," he added.

James O'Connor of Shelbourne was documented as the world-record holder following his quickfire November 1967 effort against Bohemians, but even that was rendered pedestrian in comparison when, in 2004, a new mark was belatedly recognised by the Guinness Book of Records 40 years after it took place. Tommy Ross, an 18-year-old with Highland League Ross County, scored a hat-trick in 90 short seconds against Nairn County at Victoria Park in Dingwall, although it would take 40 years for the achievement to be officially accepted as the new mark. Ross, incorrectly believing that there needed to be two timekeepers attending the game for his hat-trick to be ratified, did not make an application for it to be recorded. "Other people have been scoring hat-tricks and I have been sitting here knowing I did it in 90 seconds," Ross later explained to The Times. "This sets the record straight at last and I am totally delighted."

"Has anyone calculated how many minutes David Beckham has played for England compared to Bobby Moore? And has anyone received fewer England caps, but played more minutes than Beckham?"

The consistently excellent englandstats.com helpfully lists exactly how many minutes anyone has ever played for the national team. And yes, Billy Wright, Bobby Charlton and Bobby Moore – England's other centurions – have all played more international minutes than the Milan midfielder. Moore's 108 caps, remarkably, consist of 108 starts and he was never taken off while playing for his country. Two half-hour spells of extra-time mean Moore registered 9,780 minutes of football with England.

Beckham, in contrast, had made 101 starts and 14 substitute appearances prior to his World Cup-preventing injury of 2010. Of those 101, he has been withdrawn on 44 occasions, leaving him with a total on-pitch international career of 8,358 minutes, a full 1,422 minutes fewer than

Moore. Or, as we are feeling those long forgotten hours of GCSE maths coming back to us, works out as 15.8 whole matches. That is not to belittle Beckham's achievement; though he will struggle to overhaul the feats of the leading trio, he remains well clear of the rest. Bobby Moore: 108 caps, 9,780 minutes; Billy Wright: 105 caps, 9,480 minutes; Bobby Charlton: 106 caps, 9,439 minutes; David Beckham: 115 caps, 8,358 minutes; Bryan Robson: 90 caps, 7,649 minutes; Michael Owen: 89 caps, 6,225 minutes; Kenny Sansom: 86 caps, 7,663 minutes; Gary Neville: 85 caps, 6,827 minutes; Ray Wilkins: 84 caps, 6,930 minutes; Gary Lineker: 80 caps, 6,543 minutes; Terry Butcher: 77 caps, 6,894 minutes; Stuart Pearce: 78 caps, 6,584 minutes; John Barnes: 79 caps, 5,719 minutes; Tom Finney: 76 caps, 6,870 minutes.

"In the legendary documentary, This Is Spinal Tap, bass player Derek Smalls wears an early-80s Umbro football shirt in several scenes. Who did he support?"

The garment in question was in fact a rather fetching yellow-and-blue-striped Shrewsbury Town replica shirt from the 1980-81 season and was indeed sported by Derek Smalls, played by Harry Shearer (also known for his vocal work as Mr Burns, Ned Flanders and a host of others on The Simpsons). However, Smalls can also be seen wearing a West Ham baseball cap in the film, producing a rather unusual combination with the Shrews' shirt while visiting the grave of Elvis.

There also appears to be a case to suggest that the band's guitarist and vocalist, David St Hubbins, is a Wolves fan, given he can be spotted with a scarf that looks suspiciously like a black-and-gold Wanderers one in a few frames when the band arrive in New York for their first gig.

What is in no doubt is the reference to Kenny Dalglish made by St Hubbins in one of the film's deleted scenes. Speaking on a rooftop at their tour launch party, he tells bandmate Nigel Tufnel: "'Cause it's like you're on the top of the world here, y'know, you really are. It's like the pinnacle. Y'know it's like when Dalglish is really on his game and he's away down the field and you know he's going to take them all away, 'cause he's on top of his game, y'know. That's how I feel." Tufnel responds by claiming that Alan Hansen's wife could outrun Dalglish, prompting St Hubbins to reply: "But Dalglish, y'know, he runs the first three yards in his head." When questioned by the Guardian about the Spinal Tap reference, Dalglish readily admitted that "Marina [his wife] was certainly quicker than me in my playing days but that's not saying much. Hansen was far quicker than me, so by that I'd guess it might be about right."

"Joe Jordan scored for Scotland in three consecutive World Cup finals. Is this a record for a British player or any player?"

It is indeed a record, for no English, Welsh, or Northern Irish player has matched this feat. Come to think of it, neither has any other Scotsman. Jordan found the net against Zaire in 1974 (much good it did Scotland), Peru in 1978 (much good it did Scotland) and the USSR in 1982 (you know the routine by now). Only two men have bettered Big Joe's achievement: Pele scored for Brazil in the 1958, 1962, 1966 and 1970 tournaments, winning three titles in the process, and West Germany's Uwe Seeler did exactly the same thing, although defeat to England at Wembley was the closest he came to a winner's medal.

"I once read that in a cup final during the great famine of the 1930s, there were three Ukrainian brothers on a Kyiv team that beat their secret police-sponsored opponents from Moscow. Is it true that Stalin ordered a replay and warned the brothers to lose, only for them to defiantly win the replay before they disappeared into the gulag?"

Something very similar did occur in 1942 when Joseph Stalin sent a set of footballing siblings to the gulag, but they played for Spartak Moscow. That same year, however, members of Dynamo Kyiv's team were executed by the

Nazis after refusing to throw a series of "friendlies". But firstly the Spartak story: Nikolai, Andriy, Pyotr and Alexander Starostin, the popular brothers who led Spartak to the 1937 and 1938 USSR league championships, were illegally arrested as "enemies of the people" in the wake of their forcibly-replayed 1939 Russian Cup victory. It was the culmination of a two-decade-long vendetta against the Starostins by Lavrentiy Beria, the chief of Stalin's secret police and a former player himself, who had once been made a fool of by Nikolai during a game in the early-1920s. He was later executed in December 1953. With Stalin also dead, the Starostins were only released in 1954 when the late dictator's son, Vasili, a Spartak supporter, managed to broker their early release. Nikolai – Spartak's founder in 1922 – returned to the club and became "club leader" until his death in 1996.

Meanwhile, when Kyiv was occupied in 1941, members of the Dynamo team found work in the city's bakery No. 1 and started to play football in an empty lot. After taking up the Germans' offer of training in the Zenith Stadium, a friendly against members of the German army was suggested in 1942. The Ukrainians, who named their team FC Start, accepted and won. And they kept winning further matches, contrary to the orders of increasingly agitated German officers, prompting a game to be arranged against Flakelf, a Luftwaffe side.

This, however, is where reports of the incident become somewhat cloudy. It is widely depicted that Start won the game and defiantly won a replay, despite being threatened with severe repercussions, before a number of the team were arrested, sent to the Syrets concentration camp and subsequently executed for their contempt and refusal to lose. However, several historians suggest that the so-called "death match" has been distorted through propaganda and time; indeed, a host of conspiracy theories now surround the game, including one which suggests that a Start player had actually lined up for Flakelf. As Jonathan Wilson explained in a 2008 Guardian article, "the problem is not only that there is very little evidence, but that what evidence there is tends to be distorted. There is the Communist myth, the anti-Communist counter-myth, and between them the statements of witnesses trying to say what they think the authorities want to hear."

The legend did (loosely) inspire the 1982 film Escape To Victory, however, in which Bobby Moore, Pele and John Wark led a team of POWs to beat a crack German team and secure their freedom … even with Sly Stallone in goal.

"While browsing through the Scottish Third Division statistics for the 2000-01 season, I noticed that James McKenzie of Albion was sent off in each of the three games he had played by December. Is this a record for consecutive red cards?"

McKenzie's record is undoubtedly poor, but it can't hold a candle to the pitiful display of Dean Windass, who once managed to amass the same haul of dismissals in a mere

22 minutes during his time at Aberdeen. Having picked up a booking in the first minute of a game at Dundee United in November 1997, Windass took 21 more minutes to procure a second for another trademark industrial challenge.

Off he went. But before you could say "toy" or "pram", Windass let rip with a volley of abuse in the direction of referee Stuart Dougal, who was duly unimpressed enough by the ripe language pouring into his ears to send the bulky forward off again. Windass left the field of play in that lofty vehicle, high dudgeon, stopping awhile to rip a corner flag out of the ground and fling it to the floor like a great big bairn. Out came red card No. 3. "I don't regret any of those tackles, but hurling the corner flag was 10 seconds of madness," he offered the Sun by way of a defence. "I didn't think the first tackle even warranted a booking. I just wanted to let the lads see me get stuck in and hope it would spur them on. Of course, it all went horribly wrong."

His efforts amassed 22 penalty points, at a rate of exactly one point per minute of "action". For his trouble, he was suspended for seven weeks, while Aberdeen lost the game 5-0, a defeat which cost manager Roy Aitken his job. But the blame could not solely be aimed at Windass; the Dons were already 3-0 down before he walked. "I can't afford to let it happen again even though I know it is in my nature," he added. In 2007, after playing a game for Bradford, Windass was banned for five games after verbally abusing referee Darren Drysdale in the Valley Parade car park.

"Who was the first ever substitute in English football?"

The year was 1965, the date was 21 August and while young jivers listened to the Beatles' chart-topping hit Help! and the war began to intensify in Vietnam, Charlton Athletic's Keith Peacock became the first substitute to appear in the Football League. Peacock – father to ex-Chelsea and QPR player Gavin (who stood down from his role as a BBC pundit in 2008, emigrating to Calgary where he began a three-year religious course as preparation for his new career with the church) – achieved his footnote in football history by replacing injured keeper Mike Rose after 11 minutes of the Addicks' match at Bolton. They key word in that sentence is "injured", because during the first two seasons after the law had been introduced, a substitute – and only one was allowed then – could only come on for an injured player. From the start of the 1967-68 campaign, however, replacements were allowed to be made purely for tactical reasons.

Substitutions had been permitted on the international scene as early as the 1954 World Cup qualifiers, with West Germany's Richard Gottinger making history on 11 October 1953 against Saarland, when he came on to replace Horst Eckel in a 3-0 win. Incidentally, Saarland, a German federal state on the border of France which came under French occupation after the Second World War, had its Saarländischer Fußballbund (SFB) association founded in 1948 but never qualified for a major international tournament. Fifa only accepted Saarland as members a fortnight before the 1950 finals, while they could only finish second to West Germany in the unsuccessful qualifying campaign for the 1954 tournament. After a 3-2 defeat to Holland in their final international game in June 1956, Saarland became part of the Federal Republic of Germany and the SFB dissolved its separate Fifa membership, instead joining the German FA (Deutscher Fußball-Bund, DFB). Coach Helmut Schön went on to take charge of the West German team, winning the European Championship in 1972 and the World Cup two years later.

"In the Porridge episode, The Harder They Fall, Fletch tricks a released inmate into digging up the pitch at Elland Road. Despite a sign saying 'Leeds United FC', the ground used is not Elland Road. Does anyone know where it was filmed?"

It seems the BBC engaged in some super 70s-style technical trickery, because the stadium they used for the interior shots was QPR's Loftus Road, which is situated just around the corner from Television Centre, aligned with some exteriors of Elland Road. But Porridge's football links do not end there. Ronnie Barker's Norman Stanley Fletcher hailed from Muswell Hill and supported Tottenham; he even managed to wangle a weekend trip home from HMP Slade to see his wife but instead went to watch Spurs. However, in the film version, Fletch had switched his allegiances: "I've become disillusioned with the game – 20 years of watching Orient does that to ya."

Fletch's cellmate Lenny Godber may arrive in the first episode with a West Brom bag slung over his shoulder, but it is a red herring; he was an Aston Villa fan through and through. And Mr Mackay's allegiance is given away by Fletch in The Desperate Hours episode, when discussing the warder's views on sex: "He's a strict Presbyterian, you know. They only have sex up there when Rangers beat Celtic."

On to other 70s classics. Wolfie from Citizen Smith was a massive Fulham fan (as was the programme's writer, John Sullivan) and could often be seen wearing their scarf, although what his Marxist ideals would make of Mohamed Al-Fayed's running of the club is anyone's guess. Rigsby from Rising Damp was a supporter of Leeds United, prompting supporters at Elland Road to chant: "Rigsby is a Leeds fan, Rigsby is a Leeds fan, la la la la ..."

Bottom's Eddie Hitler signalled his allegiance when decorating his flat with "QPR" in spray-paint, while flat-mate Richie Head went one step further with the Hoops. "Isn't it true that you once did a trial for QPR?" asks Eddie, prompting Richie to reply: "That's right, actually. Yeah, Trevor Francis phones me up one day, he says: Dick Head? I said that's me." And Charlton can lay claim to being represented by Rodney from Only Fools and Horses, after Del explained to Marlene why his younger brother was so named. "Well, mum was a fan," says Del. "Of who?

Charlton Heston?" asks Marlene. "No, Charlton Athletic," deadpans Del.

"What is the record number of penalties awarded to one team in a single season?"

Manchester City were awarded an astonishing 15 spot-kicks in the 1971-72 season, all of which were scored by a grateful Francis Lee. As the official City website relates in its recollections of the campaign: "He [Lee] was prolific, scoring 35 times, 15 of these were penalties. Most of these penalties were earned by Francis himself and during this time he earned the nickname of 'Lee One Pen'."

Lee's goals were enough to propel City to fourth place with 57 points, just one point behind First Division winners Derby (and level with Leeds and Liverpool) in one of the tightest title races ever. It also secured him another nickname, "Lee Won-pen", from rival players and the Professional Game Match Officials Ltd general manager Keith Hackett, who admitted that the striker "had a reputation of falling down easily".

"Are Brighton, in 1910, the only team to have won the Charity Shield without winning either the league championship or the FA Cup?"

In a word, or six, no. In 1971, Leicester City, winners of the old Second Division, went off with the trophy. But first, a little history. When the first Charity Shield (now Community Shield) match was played in 1908, it was a professionals-versus-amateurs affair. So Manchester United, the then-reigning league champions, took on Southern League champs QPR and won. This format was continued for many years – hence Brighton's victory – but quite often was played between representative professional and amateur teams assembled on a one-off basis. The fixture was moved to coincide with the start of the new season in 1959, where it has remained a curtain-raiser ever since. But it was only in 1974 when the FA moved the game to Wembley and decreed the Shield should be a fund-raiser, contested every year between the champions and the FA Cup winners.

So what happened with Leicester? It's a simple story. Double winners Arsenal declined to enter, owing to their European commitments, and so losing Cup finalists Liverpool visited Filbert Street for what looked like an easy tie for them on paper. But in Jimmy Bloomfield's first game in charge of the Foxes, Bill Shankly's men went down to a 1-0 defeat.

"Which match holds the record for having the most red cards?"

The British league record for dismissals is five, which happened twice in 1997. First up, Division Two rivals Chesterfield and Plymouth Argyle produced a ding-dong, last-minute brawl that resulted in red cards for Spireites pair Kevin Davies and Darren Carr, plus Argyle's Tony James and Richard Logan. "The two No. 6s were having a boxing match in the net and the two No. 8s were exchanging blows outside the area," recalled referee Richard Poulain. Argyle – already reduced to 10 men by this stage – had their misery compounded by a 3-2 defeat. Then, on 2 December of that year, five more players were sent off in the Bristol Rovers v Wigan Athletic match; four got their marching orders before the break and Rovers ended up with just seven men.

According to the Guinness Book of Records, though, the most red cards dished out in a single game is an astonishing 20 and occurred in a Paraguayan second division match. With Sportivo Ameliano trailing visitors General Caballero 2-0, ref William Weiler dismissed two members of the home team; Sportivo's players did not take kindly to the decision and within moments the two sets of players were engaged in a vicious free-for-all. Eighteen more cards of a rouge nature were flourished – nine to either side – leaving just two law-abiding General Caballero players on the field. Thus, the game was abandoned.

"What was the name of the goalkeeper in the 1970s who had a plastic knuckle?"

The man you are looking for is John Osborne of West Brom, the legendary Baggies keeper who was part of a golden era in the club's history, during which time they won the 1968 FA Cup and the 1966 League Cup. Before this, however, Osborne had a plastic strip inserted in an arthritic finger, creating an extra joint and earning "Ossie" another soubriquet, "The Bionic Keeper". He sadly passed away in 1999 after battling cancer.

"What is the most prestigious match to have been decided by the toss of a coin?"

The most important coin-toss in the history of football took place in the semi-finals of the tedious 1968 European Championships. Having drawn 0-0 with the Soviet Union, Italy (led by the Internazionale defensive legend Giacinto Facchetti) progressed to the final after winning a thrilling showdown at the flick of a thumb. Meanwhile, Yugoslavia were dispatching England 1-0, thus ensuring they could be robbed in the final by the Italians. Trailing 1-0 with 10 minutes remaining, Angelo Domenghini was allowed to take a free-kick with the Yugoslavs in the process of retreating the full 10 yards. Goal, and a 1-1 draw. Italy won the replay 2-0; not exciting.

The next biggest game decided by fate took place in the 1964-65 European Cup quarter-finals, after Liverpool and Cologne played out two dour 0-0 draws and then a 2-2 play-off in Amsterdam. As referee Robert Schaut threw a red-and-white disc skywards, Ron Yeats called, only for the toss to land in the centre circle mud. Schaut repeated the process and Yeats's luck held, leaving boss Bill Shankly to comment: "They didn't deserve to lose on the toss of a coin." Liverpool were then controversially sent packing 4-3 on aggregate in the semis by Inter, led by that man Facchetti again.

But no hard-luck story is complete without Spain: they missed out on a place in the 1954 World Cup finals after beating Turkey in a two-legged qualifier, 4-2 on aggregate. Sadly, combined scores counted for nothing in those days and having won and lost a leg apiece, the teams played off. After the inevitable draw (2-2) it was, as depicted in Phil Ball's book Morbo: The Story of Spanish Football, left to a "blindfolded 14-year-old boy called Franco Gemma, who was given the task of pulling from a large silver tankard the piece of paper with the name of the team that would go to Switzerland. Of course, it said Turkey."

"Managers these days are always bleating on about playing too many games in too short a time. I'd like to know what the most congested fixture list ever is."

Like nostalgia, congestion ain't what it used to be. Back in the day, a combination of multiple Cup replays and the postponements of matches would often lead to huge clumps of fixtures at the end of a season. That is pretty rare in this age of penalty shoot-outs and undersoil heating, but there was a right old pile-up for Rangers at the back end of the 2007-08 campaign. Because of their success on four fronts, they had to play nine games in 24 days between 1-24 May, culminating in their final three league games being staged in a frantic five-day spell and prompting manager Walter Smith to fume: "What bothers me most is that the SPL has assented to every request that has been made by Celtic." Rangers ended up losing the Uefa Cup final to Zenit St Petersburg and the SPL title race to … Celtic.

Manchester United also suffered an unpleasant log-jam during two league title races in the 1990s. In the penultimate week of the 1991-92 season they played four games in eight days, from which they purloined just one point as Leeds United overhauled them on the final run-in. They had an identical schedule for the 1996-97 finale, but won the championship despite drawing the first of those games.

Congestion can also come in bitesize form, as it did in the 1960s, when three days of league football would be staged over the four days of Easter from Good Friday. Or, especially, when multiple replays were the order of the day and ties could go on longer than your average series of Lost. In 1980, when the FA Cup semi-final between Arsenal and Liverpool famously went to a third replay, the Gunners played 12 matches in a 31-day period between 5 April and 5 May, a run that took in the Cup Winners' Cup semi against Juventus to boot. On top of that, all eight of their fixtures between 12 April and 3 May took place away from home. Eventually, Arsenal prevailed in both semi-finals, but then lost the finals to West Ham and Valencia, respectively.

"I was rummaging through an old Shoot All-Star Line-Up booklet which claimed that Bobby Moore won the American League Championship with West Ham in 1963. Is this true and, if so, how was this possible?"

Think of the American League Championship (or as our cousins across the Atlantic called it, the International Soccer League) as US soccer's John the Baptist to the Major League Soccer's Jesus. For the ISL was the first post-war attempt – before the ill-fated North American Soccer League (1967-1984) and the MLS (which began in 1995) – to sell the game to the great American public. Founded in 1960 by Bill Cox, a former owner of the Philadelphia Phillies baseball team, the plan was to bring European teams across the ocean during the off-season, wow the immigrant-heavy East Coast crowds and put soccer on the map.

It nearly worked. In 1963, for instance, the ISL attracted 288,743 fans over its 42-game schedule (just under 7,000 a game). However, with most teams deciding against risking their big-name players, attendances dwindled and the ISL ground to a halt in 1965.

As for the Hammers' triumph in 1963, Moore – as you might expect – had a significant part to play. When he arrived fresh from England duty at the tournament with Johnny Byrne, West Ham were bottom of their group. But goals from Geoff Hurst – who was the tournament's leading scorer with eight – took the Hammers through to the final against Polish side Gornik, who they beat 2-1 on aggregate. Next up was an American Challenge Cup clash against the brilliant Dukla Prague side, which West Ham narrowly lost. Still, Moore's exploits were enough for him to be given the Eisenhower award as the tournament MVP and, of course, he would later return to the NASL for two spells with San Antonio Thunder and Seattle Sounders.

Incidentally, West Ham were one of nine British teams to compete in the ISL. Most notably, Kilmarnock pipped Burnley to reach the 1960 final, before losing 2-0 to Brazilian side Bangu. The following year, Everton also reached the final, only to come up against Dukla Prague and crash 9-2 on aggregate.

"Where is the most unusual place a match ball has been lost during a game (eg river, road, etc)?"

You might think a river an unusual place to lose a ball, but in some parts of the world nothing could be more natural. Take Shrewsbury, for example, where the local club's former home at Gay Meadow was situated right on the banks of the River Severn. They used to lose so many balls to the adjacent waterway that a local coracle maker – the late Fred Davies – was even employed by them to sit in one of his boats during matches and retrieve any that wound up in the water. According to the Shrews' website, "Fred is most famous for chasing a swan downstream, thinking it was a ball."

It is unlikely that any of these balls were hoofed into the Severn intentionally, unlike a number that were belted out of the Laranjeiras Stadium in the infamous 1941 Rio State Championship final between Fluminense and Flamengo. Needing only a draw to win the title, Flu took a 2-0 lead, only to be pegged back to two-apiece with seven minutes remaining. Quick-witted home players began time-wasting by lumping balls over the ground's perimeter fence and into a nearby river, although Flamengo had seemingly prepared for this ruse, having somewhat incredulously brought their rowing team to the game, and countered by sending them on a retrieval mission. Despite the rowers' best efforts, though, Flamengo were unable to score again and Flu held on to lift the trophy.

"David Healy and Eduardo were the joint top scorers in Euro 2008 qualifying, but both players' teams failed to reach the finals. Has this ever happened before?"

More often than you might think. In fact, in the last six European Championships, it has happened on four occasions. In 2004, Slovenia's Ermin Siljak banged in nine qualifying goals – more than any other player – but his team lost to Croatia in the play-offs.

In 1992, Darko Pancev scored 10 as Yugoslavia romped through Group Four, only for his country to be booted out of the finals because of UN sanctions and the emerging war in the Balkans. In 1988, the Tottenham striker Nico Claesen topped the scoring charts with seven goals for Belgium, but they still finished behind the Republic of Ireland (and Bulgaria) in their qualifying group. A respectful nod should also go to Toni Polster, who scored 11 as Austria failed to qualify for Euro 96; Davor Suker top-scored with 12.

"Which football club is the greenest?"

No, not Plymouth or Yeovil, clever clogs. We're after the likes of Dartford FC, whose £6.5m 4,100-capacity Princes Park ground has the credentials to make Al Gore go weak at the knees. The baby of spectacularly named Australian architect, Mei-yun Valdivia a L'Onions, the stadium boasts a grassed roof, solar panels to provide hot water, a small lake to catch rainwater which is then recycled, Glulam timber cladding for insulation ... even the pitch and floodlights are deliberately positioned 2m below the level of the surrounding terrain in order to reduce noise and light pollution for the neighbouring population.

And with the club turning out in the Isthmian Premier, European football – and the polluting long-haul flights that accompany it – is not an issue. Yet. Indeed, the geographical nature of the division also keeps a check on the club's carbon footprint: Dartford rarely have to travel far outside the M25, with the trips to Bognor Regis and Margate about as distant as they get. And on weekdays the car park at the ground is used as part of a park and ride service that encourages the use of public transport.

Swampy would be proud, but Dartford are by no means alone in giving environmental concerns a high priority. The City of Manchester Stadium was all set to become the first sporting arena in the world to have its own wind turbine, 360ft high, designed by Norman Foster and with the capacity to provide enough energy to power 1,250 homes. But health and safety fears that people could be injured by icicles falling from the blades scuppered the proposal. Arsenal's Emirates Stadium, however, does have excellent eco qualifications and the fact that an estimated 70% of the club's supporters use public transport to get to games gives them further brownie (or should that be greenie) points.

The Darts also have some serious competition from outside the United Kingdom. Freiburg's Dreisam Stadium has 60m^2 of solar panels, providing 60% of the club's hot water; Vitesse Arnhem's Gelredome Stadium trumps even that with 112m^2 of solar panels, 320m^2 of photovoltaic cells that generate a 30,000kWh surplus, eco-friendly cooling and heating systems, and recycled seats.

And across the pond, Charleston Battery FC are keeping their end up, declaring that they have "completed a comprehensive range of energy saving and environmental initiatives: installation of a geothermal HVAC system, adding energy-efficient hand dryers, switching out water heaters to tankless units, replacing concession beer coolers with energy-efficient models, switching incandescent bulbs with compact fluorescents, eliminating bottled water from the stadium, replacing selected urinals with waterless units and implementing a comprehensive recycling programme."

"We believe in the dangers of climate change," the Battery president Andrew Bell told us. "We host a 'Go Green' night at one of the Charleston matches each year and encourage businesses and non-profit organisations in the area to come out and showcase their green efforts and endeavours via a vendor village within the stadium. It's been very successful; we even had a bicycle-powered margarita machine one year."

"I remember Newcastle United fans invading the pitch at home to Nottingham Forest in an FA Cup sixth-round tie during their run to the final of 1974. Newcastle were trailing 3-1 and being totally outplayed at the time, but when the field was eventually cleared, Forest capitulated and lost 4-3. The FA ordered a replay at neutral Goodison Park which Newcastle subsequently won, 1-0 at the second time of asking. Have there been any other occasions where hooliganism effectively achieved its aim of turning a result in a team's favour?"

Unsavoury elements in the Club Atlético Tigre fanbase got their way in November 2009. Matias Giménez, a midfielder with the Argentinian first division club, said he would not play for the club again after criticism and a "very nasty" incident with a number of Tigre supporters. Giménez claimed he was accosted in the street on his way home from the club one day and threatened with violence over his "attitude on the pitch". Giménez added: "We argued a bit and then something very nasty happened, but I won't go into detail."

The 26-year-old then completed a move to Boca Juniors. "I took the decision for the security of my family," he explained. "They're everything to me and I don't want anything to happen to them. I have two children who really are worth more than a ball."

In November 2008, fans of the Swedish team AIK ambushed a press conference in which the club were announcing that the coach, Rikard Norling, and the chief executive, Charlie Granfelt, had been sacked. But the supporters' thirst for heads to roll remained unquenched and they shouted at the club directors, demanding that the sporting director, Ola Andersson, was fired as well. The club subsequently held a meeting and it was decided that Andersson should indeed take his leave. Within an hour, the assistant manager Nebojsa Novakovic had also jumped ship.

Staying in Stockholm, at the back end of 2009, the chairman of the parent company of Hammarby was forced to quit in the wake of darker threats from fans as the team were relegated to the second division. In his resignation letter, Staffan Thorsell wrote that "it is true that I have loved Hammarby since I was a child. But I love my wife, who I have been married to for 43 years, far more and do not want her or me to experience what we have these last days. The threats and calls for the 'death penalty' should maybe not be taken literally, but we can't close our eyes any more. I am getting threats from people in the dark when I walk home from work and my wife is afraid of who she will meet in the house on her way to the elevator."

"Have there been any recent examples of professional footballers either trialling or playing under an assumed name or pseudonym?"

We have already mentioned the case of Jay Cöppingen, aka Jürgen Klinsmann, turning out for the Orange County Blue Stars in California, but it is not even unheard of that full teams appear under an assumed name. The Dynamo Moscow outfit that faced Arsenal at Highbury on their tour of Britain in 1945 was not simply the home club of the Ministry of Interior but is believed to have been, in effect, the full national side (though Dynamo too, amid mounting scenes of paranoia, from both sides, had declared that they were facing what was, in effect, an England XI). Dynamo won 4-3.

"Have any other teams suffered as a result of 'outside agents' similar to the beach ball that scored for Sunderland against Liverpool in 2009?"

The Reds certainly were not the first to suffer in this manner, as Manchester City fans will testify. Just 12 minutes into an FA Cup fourth-round tie at Bramall Lane in 2008, a low cross from Sheffield United's Lee Martin cut a swathe through a crowd of blue and white balloons in the City six-yard box. Michael Ball air kicked as a result, allowing Luton Shelton the easiest of tap-ins. After their 2-1 defeat, City complained in writing to the FA (to no avail) over the officials' failure to clear the pitch. But, as manager Sven-Goran Eriksson earnestly admitted: "We should not blame the balloons. We should have done better."

Paul Peschisolido was another beneficiary in January 2004 during the east Midlands derby between Derby County and Nottingham Forest. The Forest goalkeeper Barry Roche fluffed a routine clearance from Wes Morgan's backpass when the ball clipped a stray paper cup just before reaching his swinging boot. As it dropped, Peschisolido volleyed home from the edge of the area to give Derby a 2-0 lead in a match they would go on to win 4-2. Peschisolido later signed the cup, which now lives out its days in the Rams' trophy cabinet.

A crucial goal in the 2008 Uefa Cup semi-final between Hamburg and Werder Bremen was also the result of outside interference. With Hamburg 1-0 up from the first leg and Werder leading 2-1 in the return match, Michael Gravgaard aimed an 83rd-minute pass towards Frank Rost in the Hamburg goal, only for the ball to bobble up after hitting a rogue ball of paper and causing the defender to shin the ball behind for a corner. From the subsequent set piece, Frank Baumann put Bremen 3-1 ahead and, despite Ivica Olic grabbing a goal back, into the final on away goals.

"You hear a lot about players' win bonuses, but which clubs have dished out unusual punishments to their players in the event of defeats?"

Plenty of managers have emphasised the stick over the carrot, some good naturedly, some in utterly unspeakable manner. In the former camp is Sam Hammam, whose Wimbledon squad in 1998-99 had a clause written into their contract that, should the Dons lose a game by five clear goals, their chairman could force them to attend an opera and eat an array of offal-based dishes at a Lebanese restaurant. "It's all in writing," admitted Robbie Earle, the Wimbledon captain at the time. "Sam can make us eat a meal which has to include sheep's testicles and all sorts of brains, intestines and horrible-sounding stuff." The threat worked, though Earle and co did come close to an ear- and taste-bud bashing when losing 5-1 to Arsenal in April 1999.

It seems bizarre punishments were very much de rigeur in 1998-99 when, as detailed in the Journal du Soir, 11 players of Burkino Faso army side Armed Forces Sporting Union had their heads shaved and were thrown in jail for the night after losing a decisive game. "It's true that it was only football but the people concerned must realise that they are soldiers and playing football in the army is not simply sport but is a mission," said the club president, Commander Zoumana Traoré. "If I had them shaved it is to show that every time they have to defend the army's honour they must undertake their task with all seriousness."

In 2000, an Ivory Coast squad containing Olivier Tebily and Ibrahima Bakayoko were detained in an army camp by the military following their exit from the African Nations Cup, the government apparently claiming it was for the players' protection lest angry fans had sought reprisals.

But the most disturbing case is undoubtedly that of Uday Hussein, Saddam's son, who was placed in charge of the Iraqi Olympic Committee and, therefore, the national side. Punishments – for they seem to have been brutally dished out almost at random – included beatings with electrical cables, being forced to kick a concrete ball and having their feet scalded and toenails pulled out. As Suzanne Goldenberg reported in the Guardian in 2003, "footballers say he never really understood or showed much interest in the game itself, but was desperate enough for a win that he would phone up the dressing room during half-time to threaten to cut off the players' legs and throw them to ravenous dogs. As football overseer, Uday kept a private torture scorecard, with written instructions on how many times each player should be beaten on the soles of his feet after a particularly poor showing."

Sharar Haydar, a former Iraqi international, had an even more horrific tale. "One time, after a friendly against Jordan in Amman that we lost 2-0, Uday had me and three team-mates taken to the prison," he told Sports Illustrated. "When we arrived, they took off our shirts, tied our feet together and pulled our knees over a bar as we lay on our backs. Then they dragged us over pavement and concrete, pulling the skin off our backs. Then they pulled us through a sandpit to get sand in our backs. Finally, they made us climb a ladder and jump into a vat of raw sewage. They wanted to get our wounds infected. The next day, and for every day we were there, they beat our feet. My punishment, because I was a star player, was 20 [lashings] per day." Uday Hussein was killed in a gunfight with US troops in 2003.

"Having witnessed Chris Kirkland sport a rather natty cap to shield his eyes from the sun, have there been any outfield players who preferred headwear while playing? Would this even be legal?"

First things first. According to the game's rulebook, outfield players simply are not allowed to wear caps, though goalkeepers may. Yet it does appear that they may wear other forms of headgear. Take the Petr Cech-style skullcap, also sported by the Charlton centre-back Miguel Ángel Llera. Such protection could also be seen on the Northern Ireland international Tommy Priestley, who played for Chelsea in the 1930s, though it is understood he merely used it to cover up his baldness.

Another variant could be seen on the head of the former Nigeria international Efe Sodje, who wore a coloured bandana matching his kit (his mother believed it would help ward off evil spirits) for more than a decade at nine different English league clubs, finishing with Bury. When Shakers fans began snapping them up from the club shop in 2008, Sodje admitted: "It gives me a lift and I see it as a big honour."

Yet even Sodje must tip his, er, bandana, to Charlie Athersmith, winger for Aston Villa, Small Heath and England at the turn of the 20th century. Midlands myth has it that, during one icily bitter 1901 Villa match against Sheffield United, in which a number of players suffered mild frostbite from the sheeting sleet, Athersmith simply used his head and put it under an umbrella he had borrowed from a fan for the remainder of the game.

"Other than the obvious Cantona kung-fu kick, are there many other examples of players attacking supporters, in particular their own?"

Eric Cantona and his Selhurst Park shenanigans are by no means alone in their aggressive attitude towards supporters. Take the Colombian midfielder Javier Flórez, who went too far after losing in a local tournament final in 2009. The Atletico Junior player shot into a group of supporters – killing one – who chanted "weak, weak, weak" at him as he drove past. Flórez explained he was "drunk and angry" when it happened, following his release from prison on £45,000 bail, before adding rather incredibly: "He really upset me, but I repent in my heart. I just hope people know what I have suffered." Flórez was convicted of manslaughter, sentenced to three years' probation and returned to the Atletico Junior team in January 2010.

Somewhat less tragic, thankfully, is the story of Gerry Armstrong, who clambered into the Brighton stands during a Sussex Cup tie for the club's reserves against Southwick in January 1988, apparently riled by remarks from spectator Wayne Marmont after receiving the first red card of his career. "I couldn't help myself," said Armstrong. "The damage was done before I realised what had happened." Marmont required six stitches in a gashed forehead, Armstrong left the Seagulls a fortnight later and, after a court appearance on a charge of causing grievous bodily harm, was conditionally discharged for a year and ordered to pay £200 compensation and £20 costs.

Major League soccer supporters also seem to inflame players' ire. David Beckham confronted Los Angeles Galaxy fans in, admittedly, what was little more than a stare-down, in 2009, and Clint Mathis was fined $500 for a similar incident in 2003. Neither, though, could be construed as an outright attack, unlike the case of Tampa Bay's Mamadou Diallo, MLS's top goalscorer in 2000 who, according to Colorado director of public relations Mark Saunders, lunged towards and threw "a right overhand roundhouse punch" at a Rapids fan as he walked off the pitch at full-time following a 2-1 defeat. The supporter, who Diallo accused of racial abuse, apparently held off his attacker with the help of an umbrella. Diallo was handed a four-game suspension, a $5,000 fine and ordered to go on an anger-management course.

Another player whose feathers were ruffled by a member of the crowd was Romario, who ended up fighting

Ricardo Gomes during a Fluminense training session in the autumn of 2003. Fed up with the Romario's form for Flu, Gomes fired a torrent of abuse at him and then six chickens to boot, prompting the inevitable set-to. "You're not going to give me a bollocking in my own home?" fumed the striker. "No, you're not, are you. If you want to have a go at me, go to the Maracana, but don't do it here." Gomes later told reporters: "He can't play football, but he knows how to fight." Sadly, the brawl was not without its casualties: one member of the poultry weapon died.

Mind, it isn't just players who have dealt out their own brand of fan justice. Brian Clough took less than kindly to the Nottingham Forest supporters that invaded the pitch during a match with QPR in January 1989 and waded in to smack some sense into as many of them as he could lay his hands on. "He clipped me round the ear, then kept on going and hit other people," recalled Paul Richardson, one of the fans on the end of Clough's right hand. "The stewards just stood back and let him get on with it." One MP demanded that he "should be prosecuted and banned from games like any other yob", but the FA made do with handing out a £5,000 fine and touchline ban, while Clough later apologised to Richardson and gave him tickets to that year's Littlewoods Cup final.

"After reading that Ipswich and Republic of Ireland Under-21 goalkeeper Shane Supple walked away from football at the age of just 22, can you tell us of any other players who have turned their back on the beautiful game?"

"I suppose you could say that I have fallen out of love with the game and when that happens I've always said to myself that I wouldn't hang around," said Supple in August 2009 following his decision to retire and swap his No. 1 jersey for a chef's apron. "People probably think I'm crazy, but I'm not going to stay in the game for anyone else." But Supple isn't the first bright young thing to seek satisfaction away from the sport.

Peter Knowles was a young attacking midfielder and, despite struggling with injuries, a vital cog in Wolves's 1966-67 promotion from the Second Division. After earning England Under-23 honours during the following season, he had an outside chance of making the 1970 World Cup squad, but by the summer of '69 Knowles's priorities had changed. "I shall continue playing football for the time being but I have lost my ambition," he said. "Though I still do my best on the field, I need more time to learn about the Bible and may give up football." Eight league games later he did just that, choosing to follow his beliefs as a Jehovah's Witness. Wolves would optimistically hold on to his registration until finally releasing him on a free transfer in 1982, while Billy Bragg would later be inspired by Knowles's story to write the song, God's Footballer

("He scores goals on a Saturday / And saves souls on a Sunday").

The New England Revolution player Chase Hilgenbrinck also hung up his boots to choose the pulpit over the pitch, leaving the MLS in 2008 to become a Catholic priest. "I felt called to something greater," he said. "At one time I thought that call might be professional soccer. In the past few years, I found my soul is hungry for something else."

Religion also accounted for the career of former Argentina and Real Mallorca goalkeeper Carlos Roa. In the summer of 1999, Roa, a Seventh-day Adventist, retired. "The issue of Saturday, the Sabbath, the seventh day, is the main reason why I am leaving professional soccer," he said. "For the people of God and for those who respect His Word, this is a very special day, and soccer does not allow me to do what I must do on that day." After a year spent in a New Mexico countryside retreat, Roa flip-flopped (although, as he informed FourFourTwo, he continued to abstain from football on Saturdays) and returned to Mallorca, but struggled to recapture his best form, drifting down the divisions – and battling testicular cancer – before becoming the goalkeeping coach for Constancio del Inca in the Balaeric Third Division.

The former Tottenham keeper and member of Norway's 1998 World Cup squad Espen Baardsen was another man between the sticks that chose to quit the game early, at the age of 25. "I got bored of it," he told the Observer. "Once you've played in the Premier League and been to the World Cup, you've seen it and done it. It was dictating what I could do and when. I felt unsatisfied intellectually, I wanted to travel the world." The final straw, it would seem, came when the then Sheffield United manager Neil Warnock offered Baardsen "less than what a tube driver earns". He went on to work for an asset management company – after travelling the globe for 18 months. Another Spurs player, Rory Allen, also turned his back on football prematurely, leaving instead to watch the 2002 Ashes series in Australia. "It was an amazing experience," declared Allen, even though England lost 4-1.

Hidetoshi Nakata, the Japan midfielder who retired after the 2006 World Cup aged 29, offered up "it was just my time to quit" as his rather enigmatic explanation. He too chose to travel ("I've visited a hundred countries, but there are still plenty more," he told Fifa.com in 2008), as well as becoming editor-at-large of Monocle, "more of a book than a magazine ... a global briefing covering international affairs, business, culture and design".

Liverpool's versatile Australian, Craig Johnston, writer of the Anfield Rap, chose to retire in the summer of 1988 and care for his seriously ill sister. "I have been playing football since I arrived in this country as a 14-year-old triallist," he said. "But there's more to life than soccer." Graeme Souness tried to tempt him back to the club in 1991, but the player preferred to focus on other interests, chief among them the invention of the Adidas Predator boot (Johnston's follow-up, the Pig, made the shortlist of four for the 2004 Designer of the Year award; it lost) and a minibar security system (The Butler), as well as designing a brand of surfboard, creating game show The Main Event, setting up his own soccer school and launching a career as a photographer in Florida.

"Ah fuck it! I'm away," were the immortal words with which George Connelly, once dubbed the Scottish Franz Beckenbauer, ended his career aged 26. The teenage Connelly appeared to have the world at his feet when making his mark in the Celtic first team in the aftermath of the Lisbon Lions team, but his frequent walkouts were a sign of things to come. In a Sunday Herald interview in 2006, he explained: "I was going home with £59 a week. It was costing me money to play football. I had a house to buy, a mortgage to pay, I had two kids, two cars, the gas and the electric bills, and a marriage that wasn't working, so what was the point?" Admittedly exercising "drink-fuelled logic", Connelly was offered a trial by Tommy Docherty at Manchester United, but "took a job lagging pipes in Grangemouth" instead. "It paid £115 a week after tax, more than I earned at the peak of my career," he wrote in his autobiography, Celtic's Lost Legend. He later became a taxi driver and married for the second time.

Another lost talent was Robin Friday, "the game's first rock star" and "the greatest footballer you never saw", as Paolo Hewitt described him in the Guardian. Friday lived just as hard as he played the game, "smoked spliffs, dropped pills, drank heavily and accommodated every woman that came his way". After leaving Reading for Cardiff (he was arrested for dodging the train fare on the way), Friday famously got sent off for kicking Brighton's Mark Lawrenson in the face before breaking into the opponents' dressing room and defecating in his victim's bag. He walked out in the summer of 1977, claiming he'd had enough of people telling him what to do. Friday returned to London, where he died of a suspected heroin overdose 12 years later. The Super Furry Animals would later release the single, The Man Don't Give A Fuck, with Friday flicking a V sign to the Luton keeper Milija Aleksic while playing for Cardiff on the front cover. Its sleeve notes read: "This record is dedicated to the memory of Robin Friday, 1952 to 1990, and his stand against the 'Man'."

"I noticed that Stoke's players have been using computer games to help with team bonding and communication. Are there any other examples of clubs using such games to improve their chances?"

The Potters players in question had actually been fuelling their team spirit with nightly web-based Gears of War and Call of Duty sessions. "It sounds stupid but we communicate just like we do on the pitch," said Stoke combatant Liam Lawrence in 2009. "We talk online at night in exactly the same way. Even the old ones get involved; it's a good laugh and something to do when you have to stay in at night and be good."

Going back more than two decades, we can point to a side that used rather more archaic computer games, but whether they truly boosted their chances is somewhat open to debate. The 1988 Soviet Union European Championship team was, as recounted in Simon Kuper's excellent 1994 book Football Against the Enemy, selected on the back of players' results in a number of computer games or tests created by the Kyiv scientist Anatoly Zelentsov. "There were 40 candidates [for the squad]," said Zelentsov, "and with these tests we selected the first 20."

The games, also used to deduce prospective signings' suitability for the Dynamo Kyiv side of the time, tested a range of attributes from nerve and endurance to reaction times and memory. "There are lots of ways of testing," added Zelentsov. "But I prefer the computer." With some justification – the Soviet side reached the Euro 88 final before Marco van Basten's videogame-like volley set the Dutch on their way to glory.

More recently, the best-selling Football Manager series has also been employed by several clubs. "We started getting phone calls from scouts," Miles Jacobson, the managing director of Sports Interactive, the game's developers, told The Times in 2006. "Someone Ray [Houghton, the former Republic of Ireland midfield player, an adviser on the game] worked with called us up and said, 'We've been called by a club in Division One, they need a left-back, we can't come up with any and we thought you might know about some kids'. He sent a fax with some details; 20 minutes later, having done a database search, I sent him a list of 30 players and three weeks later I saw in the paper that one of those had signed for the club. We did that!"

According to Jacobson, Peter Taylor's sole England squad for the November 2000 friendly with Italy so flummoxed opposing coach Giovanni Trapattoni that he needed extra, unconventional, help. "There was Trapattoni on the coach looking at the England squad, going, 'I've never heard of any of these players'," recalled Jacobson. "So Demetrio Albertini gets out his laptop, boots up the game and starts going through the players to show Trapattoni what they were like."

"What is the current record crowd for a friendly in Britain?"

Pleasantly straightforward, this one. The record for an international friendly is 125,683 – achieved at Hampden Park for a game between Scotland and France, which the home side won 2-0 in April 1949. The club friendly record attendance stands at 104,493 for Rangers 1-2 Eintracht Frankfurt, also at Hampden, in October 1961.

An honourable mention goes to Chelsea 3-3 Dynamo Moscow in 1945. While the official attendance was listed as 85,000, many witnesses estimated the true figure to be closer to six figures. The highest official gate for Dynamo's tour was actually at Ibrox, however, where 92,000 crammed in to watch them draw with Rangers.

"Which teams have been involved in dust-ups during meaningless exhibition matches?"

A fair few, would be the short answer, and we have already covered testimonials gone bad in the first edition of the Knowledge, but several stand-out friendly examples do spring to mind, none more so than QPR's infamous "great brawl of China" fracas in 2007. The Chinese Olympic team had been holding a two-week training camp in England, from which seven players had to be sent home after a fight that involved almost every player on the pitch, plus a number of coaches and bystanders.

"I've never seen anything like it in my life," one witness told the Ealing Gazette at the time. "There were punches, kung-fu kicks and all sorts. It was absolute mayhem." China's Zheng Tao was knocked out and suffered a fractured jaw in the melee, and QPR were later fined £20,000, with assistant manager Richard Hill suspended for three months.

But while that set-to took place on a muddy training field, Thailand and Qatar held their own epic brawl live on national TV back in 1998. Qatar's players had reacted badly to a decision by referee Ekchai Thanatdeunkhao early in the second half, disputing it for more than five minutes before one Thai player came over to complain about the delay. He got shoved in the chest and then all hell broke loose. The game was eventually abandoned, after a series of running battles involving both sets of players and even one or two journalists, who reportedly began "throwing debris from the sidelines".

Falkirk's pre-season encounter with Turkish side Rizespor during their Dutch tour of 2006 ended equally abruptly after a series of skirmishes on and off the pitch. Relations between the sides got off to a bad start after Rizespor showed up at 5.37pm for a match that had been scheduled to kick off at 3pm (citing 'medical grounds' in the warm July conditions), and the officials then walked off the field after 22 minutes when a scuffle broke out in the Falkirk penalty area. They were persuaded to return and Rizespor scored soon afterwards. When Falkirk equalised in the second half, however, Rizespor's goalkeeper Atilla Koca took exception to the celebrations of Bairns fans behind his goal – among them a streaker – and quickly became embroiled in a fight with a number of them. The match was swiftly abandoned.

Most recently, Newcastle United's 2009 pre-season friendly at Huddersfield descended into an ugly 20-man brawl after a confrontation between Habib Beye and Town's skipper Peter Clarke. Always one to look on the brighter side of things after his team's 1-0 win, then-Magpies caretaker manager Chris Hughton said: "Sometimes it's nice to have that bit of edge on the pitch. You would rather have a game where the players care, and that is what happened with that incident."

"Who is the world's youngest ever professional footballer?"

Mauricio Baldivieso, a striker with Aurora in the Bolivian league, was sent on as a 39th-minute substitute in a first division match against La Paz in July 2009. Three days before his 13th birthday. Although it reportedly all ended in tears, the result of some rough marking from the La Paz defence, the player's coach – the former Bolivia midfielder Julio César Baldivieso (helpfully, also Mauricio's father) – offered the following impartial assessment of his son's ability: "I'm very proud, he's got a lot of talent." According to reports in South America, Baldivieso beat a record set by Peru's Fernando García, who turned out for Juan Aurich in 2001 aged just 13.

It is, however, all but impossible to verify the age of some other whipper-snappers who may have bounded out in the men's game before their voices had broken. The former Manchester United youngster Souleymane Mamam, for instance, is still listed by Fifa as the youngest-ever player in a World Cup qualifying match, supposedly aged 13 years and 310 days when he appeared for Togo against Zambia in May 2001. Presumably this was not his senior debut, meaning it is possible he was close to Baldivieso's age when he first stepped out, although question marks have continued to hover over Mamam's claims throughout his career. When he appeared for Royal Antwerp on loan from United, for instance, the club listed his year of birth as 1985, meaning he was at least 16 at the time of the Togo-Zambia match in question.

The Ghana-born United States international Freddy Adu first attracted the attentions of the Washington Post when he was but 12 years old, and there was much Adu in the Sports Illustrated in 2003 when the striker was 13. He had to wait until 14 to sign a professional contract at DC United, though, and was two months shy of 15 when he made his full debut.

That makes Adu barely younger than the youngest-ever verified Football League player: the Barnsley striker Reuben Noble-Lazarus, who was 15 years and 45 days old when he appeared against Ipswich Town on a Tuesday night in September 2008 (he was back at Newsome High School in Huddersfield the next morning). As for the English top flight, Fulham's defender Matthew Briggs is the youngest to ever grace Premier League turf. He was 16 years and 65 days old when he came on as a substitute in May 2007 but, at the time of writing, has yet to make a first-team appearance since.

"In the early 90s, Farnborough Town were sponsored by indie band Mega City Four. At around the same time, Clydebank were backed by soggy, Scottish balladeers Wet Wet Wet, while in recent years, Norman Cook's label Skint has lent its name to Brighton and Hove Albion's shirt. Have any other football clubs been sponsored by bands, groups, musicians or labels?"

Leaving aside the musicians who have been involved as shareholders on a board level at clubs – such as Elton John at Watford and Robbie Williams at Port Vale, for example – there have been plenty of other bands and labels putting their money where their hearts lie.

After borrowing their name from the former club of ex-Leeds United defender Lucas Radebe, the Kaiser [sic] Chiefs thought they ought to give something back. When the club signed Tore Andre Flo in 2007, the band sponsored the player. "We just thought it would be a good thing to do to show our support and try and do something for the club," said bassist Simon Rix.

Back in 2004, Welsh rappers Goldie Lookin' Chain lent their names to Newport County AFC for their run in the Football Association of Wales Premier Cup. So it was that, as the club ran out for their first match against Caernarfon, they wore bright gold shirts, emblazoned with GLC and complete with a delicate gold medallion motif around their necks. Band member Mike Balls said their contribution to the shirt design, however, was minimal. "It was just towards the actual medallion vibe," he admitted.

Five years earlier in 1999, another Welsh band, Super Furry Animals, also put their weight behind Cardiff City's FAW Cup campaign after agreeing a five-figure shirt deal. The players themselves were nonplussed. "Once you get the shirt on, you tend to forget about it," said striker Kevin Nugent.

Over in Germany, Die Toten Hosen sponsored their local team Fortuna Düsseldorf to the tune of around £400,000 when they dropped down to amateur league level, helping to keep the club afloat before they returned to professional football. The punk rockers are no longer listed as an official sponsor, but the club shop still sells an official Die Toten Hosen F95 Kollektion, while the youth teams still turn out with the band's logo on their shirt.

In 1996, Margate FC managed to persuade music label Link Music to sponsor the side, leading to Bad Manners singer and renowned gourmand Buster Bloodvessel not only becoming a board member but also splashing the name of his band across their shirts. It obviously worked, an unbeaten run of 14 matches helped the club to their best finish in nine years. Indie label Cherry Red Records also has a proud history of being involved in lower-league football, having sponsored both the Hellenic League and Kingstonian FC, the team who carried the name of their local high-street record store, Banquet Records, on their chests.

Dropping down to junior level, Rowsley Sunday League team, Park Hall Rangers FC were sponsored by Irish boyband Boyzone back in 1997-98. "Our manager, Dave Mannion, had contacts within the rally driving industry who happened to know band member Shane Lynch," explained team member Liam Bradley. "He and the rest of Boyzone agreed to provide us with our football strips, much to the bemusement/amusement of opposition teams who would often 'take the preverbial' before kick-off and sing a medley of Boyzone hits to us. One particular game, this heavily backfired on the opposition, who despite being 4-0 up at half-time, ended up 5-4 losers. I then experienced the surreal prospect of a post-game congratulatory chat with Shane himself, who proceeded to invite me backstage along with two other lucky team-mates to meet Boyzone after one of their world tour gigs."

But perhaps the greatest ever music-based sponsorship deal was struck by the manager of another boys' side, Greenbank Under-10s B Team from Lincoln. In 2006, their opponents were no doubt stunned to see the lads run out to the strains of Motörhead's Ace of Spades, while sporting shirts decorated by the band's famous Snaggletooth skull logo. "I knew Lemmy years ago," said the team's manager Gary Weight. "I think the thought of a football team running out with the Motörhead logo made him chuckle a bit, so that's where it's come from. The hope is that we can go out on the football pitch and terrorise the opponents ..."

"I'm sure when I was a kid, I was watching Saint and Greavsie and they had a feature on the former Manchester City idol David White. I'm sure they mentioned him having a second job working at a rubbish tip. Is this true? And if it is, are there any other strange second jobs footballers have had?"

Perhaps most famously, Stuart Pearce was a trained electrician and when he joined Nottingham Forest he advertised his services in the matchday programme (he also worked as a plumber during his formative years at Wealdstone). Second jobs were a more common occurrence in those sepia-tinged pre-Premier League days – Neil Warnock, for example, as well as being a trained chiropodist, also ran a fruit and veg stall in Sheffield market.

Across the pond, there's Troy Perkins, who in 2006 was not just first-choice goalkeeper for DC United and a pick for the MLS All-Star team, but a mortgage loan processor, leading fans to greet him with the banner: "Troy saves – and loans".

Mat Mitchell-King has, for now at least, given up his career in modelling – and celebrity body doubling – after signing for Crewe Alexandra. "My first job was for Armani," said the former Histon player. "I thought I was going to be a millionaire in my first year, but it didn't work out like that. I am Rio Ferdinand's official body double. I think my rates are a bit cheaper than his."

And then, of course, there is the France striker Steve Savidan, who combined life on the pitch with refuse collection off it. During his part-time playing days with Angoulême, Savidan worked, among other things, as a binman to supplement his income.

But what of David White, you may (or may not) ask? "The truth is that, when David was a footballer, he spent some afternoons working in the office of my business, White Reclamation Ltd," his father, Stewart, told us via email. "Although there is a connection to rubbish tips, [it] is actually a waste recycling company based in Eccles, Manchester and is now, probably, the largest privately-owned waste recycling business in the north of England.

"Upon his retirement through injury at the age of 30, David joined the company full-time. That was in 1997 and he has now succeeded me as managing director. As a matter of interest, we traced your [original online] article because our company website had over 700 hits on one day in July and we couldn't understand why, so we had our people investigate and it led us to you."

"How much were the players participating in Euro 2008 paid? And who paid them?"

Uefa sold the advertising and TV rights for the tournament and distributed some of the revenue to the respective FAs. Each individual FA then determined how much to pass on to its players which, for most countries, was a relatively small amount in comparison with club salaries. However, many teams were also offered significant bonuses as a reward for progressing.

The German Soccer Federation (DFB), for example, would have handed over a €250,000 bonus to each player had they won the tournament – €50,000 less than if they had won the 2006 World Cup. They did, however, receive €150,000 for reaching the final. Spanish players, on the other hand, each picked up €214,000 for winning the trophy, but would have only got €30,000 had they failed to progress beyond the group stage. Marca later reported, however, that the victorious players would receive an increased bonus of €500,000 and – rather strangely – a state-of-the-art television.

Hefty rewards offered by the controversial Steaua Bucharest owner Gigi Becali, however, were turned down by the Romanian Football Federation (FRF). He offered €500,000 for players and staff if Romania reached the quarter-finals and €5.5m were they to win the tournament, though this was flatly rejected, the FRF general director Ionut Lupescu pointedly declaring: "We don't need any bonus from Becali, who could invest his money to improve Steaua's performance." Eventually, two other local businessmen stepped in and offered €600,000 to each of the players had they fought their way into the last eight. Not that they needed to empty their wallets, as it turned out.

For what it is worth, England players would have earned £250,000 per man had they won the tournament. Incredibly, they were still reported to have pocketed six-figure sums for failing to even qualify. According to the Daily Mail, the FA used money from sponsors to pay the players according to how many qualifying games they featured in, although the organisation's spokesman said: "We don't discuss player payments and wouldn't make any comment on any potential bonuses." Generously, the England players now donate their £1,500 match fees to charity.

"What is the strangest reason for an internal club suspension?"

While many people view Strictly Come Dancing as a crime on their eyes, Mohun Bagan took particular exception to their skipper Bhaichung Bhutia participating in the Indian version, Jhalak dikhla Ja, in 2009. Rightly piqued at the 32-year-old's dance practice repeatedly coming before training and even an exhibition match, the I-League club suspended him for six months. "If they think I am not professional enough and that I have done something wrong, why do they still want me at the club?" an angry Bhutia told DNA. "This is no way of treating someone, especially a person who has served Indian football for so long." The former Bury player went on to terminate his Mohun Bagan contract and, as if to rumba all over their pain, he ended up winning the series too.

Among other instances, there is also the case of Saudi legend Saeed al-Owairan, he of the 1994 World Cup goal of the tournament, who was punished for a decadent Western lifestyle which contravened the strict Islamic law of his nation. First up, he left his club, Al Shabab, without permission for a two-week holiday in Morocco in 1995. Then, early the following year, he was spotted by the Saudi police cavorting with a group of women – including some non-Saudis – and flung in jail.

"It wasn't like a jail, jail," said a surprisingly chipper al-Owairan at a later date. "It was a detention centre and I was held for questioning for several weeks." Other reports claimed al-Owairan was undercooking the story slightly, and that his incarceration lasted for "a little longer than six months". The player was eventually released, and though he would be banned from football for a year, he did represent Saudi Arabia again, at the 1998 World Cup.

"Has a team ever gone a whole season undefeated but failed to win the league?"

Perugia dodged defeat in the 1978-79 Serie A season, but they also avoided victory in 19 of their 30 matches, enabling Milan to pip them to the title. This dubious achievement can also be claimed by four other teams in major European leagues: in 1951, Spartak Sofia finished a point behind CDNV Sofia, despite winning 14 and drawing eight of their 22-game programme; Benfica were the next unfortunates, losing out on goal difference to Porto in 1977-78; after Perugia's antics, Galatasaray joined the select band of clubs experiencing this type of frustration, trailing home Besiktas on goal difference in 1985-86 after a 36-match unbeaten streak; and in 2008, Red Star Belgrade finished a whopping five points behind their city rivals Partizan after 33 games of mellow fruitlessness.

The best example Britain has to offer is Rangers' doomed domestic campaign of 1967-68. Going into the last match of the season, the Gers were unbeaten and level on points with Celtic, only to lose 3-2 at home to Aberdeen; three days later, Celtic won 2-1 at Dunfermline to win the title. Then again, Davie White's side had gone into the final round of games trailing the Bhoys' goal average by a country mile and would have needed a miracle to overcome this. It is worth sparing a thought for White who, having come so close to wresting the title from Jock Stein's reigning European champions, guided the team to a Fairs Cup semi-final and quarter-final, and a Scottish Cup final, only to lose them all and be turfed out on his ear in November 1969, the first Rangers manager never to win a major trophy. It was an unwanted record he would hold until the arrival of Paul Le Guen.

"Are Milan the first club to retire a number as a mark of respect for a player's retirement as they have done for Franco Baresi?"

Far from it, though it is worth noting that Milan have already semi-retired Paolo Maldini's No. 3 shirt, which the player has given permission to the club should either of his sons play for the *Rossoneri*.

Dozens of clubs around the world have retired shirt numbers, either posthumously or in tribute to their careers, but the most famous case is surely an unsuccessful attempt: the Argentinian Football Federation decided to pension off Diego Maradona's iconic No. 10 shirt in 2001, and submitted their 23-man squad list for the 2002 World Cup numbered 1 to 24, with the 10 omitted. The list was flung back in their face, Fifa telling them to do it properly and Sepp Blatter even suggesting that third-choice goalkeeper Roberto Bonano fill the shirt so that "this time Argentina's No. 10 would be able to use his hands". Argentina did not see the funny side, but eventually presented a list with Ariel Ortega at No. 10.

Several clubs in England have retired a number permanently, but most as a result of a player's sudden death. Hartlepool (Michael Maidens, No. 25), Manchester City (Marc-Vivien Foé, No. 23), QPR (Ray Jones, No. 31) and Wycombe (Mark Philo, No. 14) have all withdrawn them in the wake of a tragedy. Elsewhere, Chelsea's No. 25 shirt has been left unused in tribute to Gianfranco Zola's stellar Stamford Bridge career, while West Ham left 15 years between Bobby Moore's death in 1993 and the announcement of their No. 6 shirt's withdrawal.

Perhaps the nicest story is Ferencvaros's retirement of their No. 1 shirt in honour of Gyula Grosics. The legendary Hungarian goalkeeper wanted to sign for the club in the 1960s, but was refused permission to do so by the communist regime running the country at the time. In 2008, that wrong was at least partially righted when the club signed the 82-year-old, let him kick off in a friendly against Sheffield United and stand in goal for a few minutes, before retiring his shirt. The 1954 World Cup runner-up is still technically a player for the club.

"I stumbled upon evidence of the 1970-71 FA Cup third-and-fourth-place play-off between Everton and Stoke. I never knew these games existed. Were they played every season and when were they introduced/scrapped?"

They were staged every season from 1970, but only for five years after proving unpopular with players and fans alike. The FA even experimented with holding the game in August – shortly before the beginning of the following season – in 1972 and 1973, but this failed to win over the doubters, and the last such play-off was held on 9 May 1974, with Burnley winning 1-0 against Leicester City.

The play-off did produce one significant first, however. Birmingham's victory on penalties after a 0-0 draw against Stoke on 5 August 1972 was the first time any FA Cup tie had been decided on spot-kicks.

"Brentford were promoted to League One in 2008-09 without their manager winning a single manager-of-the-month award, nor a single player 'good enough' to get in the division's PFA team of the season. Is this combination unique?"

It appears to be the case, simply because no other manager has missed out on this prize for an entire season while leading their team to promotion. As for the PFA team of the season, champions have been overlooked around 10 times down the years, though it's only happened on one other occasion since 1990. The full list of other sides comprises: Bury (third tier, 1996-97), Bristol Rovers (third tier, 1989-90), Millwall (second tier, 1987-88), Swindon (fourth tier, 1985-86), Chesterfield (fourth tier, 1984-85), QPR (second tier, 1982-83 – second-placed Wolves, who finished 10 points behind, had four), Wimbledon (fourth tier, 1982-83), Leicester (second tier, 1979-80), Shrewsbury (third tier, 1978-79) and Mansfield (third tier, 1976-77).

Conversely, eight is the record number of players from one team filling the PFA's team, set by Manchester United in 2006-07 (Edwin van der Sar, Gary Neville, Rio Ferdinand, Nemanja Vidic, Patrice Evra, Ryan Giggs, Paul Scholes and Cristiano Ronaldo) and West Ham in 1980-81 (Phil Parkes, Ray Stewart, Alvin Martin, Billy Bonds, Trevor Brooking, Alan Devonshire, Paul Goddard and David Cross).

"Once, as he prepared his team for a match in the dressing room, ex-Croatia national coach Miroslav Blazevic took his new Rolex, dropped it, jumped on it and then said: 'I want you to smash them like I smashed this watch'. Are there any stranger examples of unorthodox motivational techniques used by managers?"

There is one particular case from Carlton Palmer's stint as manager of Stockport County which is more than worthy of a mention. In March 2002, County found themselves 20 points adrift at the bottom of what is now the Championship, helped in no part whatsoever by the fact they had failed to win a game in daylight for almost a year. To recreate the atmosphere of a night-time game – all their victories that season had come on Tuesday evenings – Palmer had the bright idea of turning on the floodlights during afternoon matches, no matter how sunny the day, and also having the dressing room windows blacked out.

"We need to do something, and maybe changing the players' body clocks so they think it's a night game will help," said Steve Bellis, County's rather optimistic marketing manager at the time. "We won't be having pre-match lunches. We'll be having post-match dinners instead." Remarkably, Stockport did go on to win three of their last four home games, but it was too late: they were relegated with just 26 points, 22 behind their nearest rivals.

There is also the charming tale of Roberto Fernandes, the coach of Brazilian team Figueirense, who would make players that were not pulling their weight in training wear pink dresses. Although the squad claimed to agree with the policy, others were not so sure. "The same rules of respect towards the dignity of a person apply to ordinary workers just as they do to soccer players," said Cezar Britto, the president of the Brazilian Association of Lawyers.

"When Robbie Savage was invited on to the flight deck during a trip home from Finland in 2007, the pilot's career was effectively ended after he was disciplined for breaking anti-terror rules. Are there any other examples of footballers ending other people's careers off the pitch?"

The short answer is no. However, it would be remiss of us not to revisit this Robbie Savage tale which, it transpires, took place as the Welshman was returning with Blackburn from Finland on a private charter flight, when he got the call to join Cpt Pablo Mason. When airline MyTravel got wind of the "scandal", however, Cpt Mason took the fall and was sacked for gross misconduct.

"Yes, I broke a rule. I did interpret the rule wasn't quite as strict for a private charter, which this was," explained Cpt Mason. "Everyone on board knew each other. I think, above all, his [Savage's] anxiety about flying has been relaxed in some way." A MyTravel spokesman replied: "We have a zero-tolerance policy towards any actions which could endanger the safety of our passengers and employees."

Cpt Mason, a former RAF pilot, launched a claim for unfair dismissal, but his wings were clipped again in March 2009 when an employment tribunal ruled that the airline had acted within its rights. "I can't not be a pilot," he complained. "I feel totally privileged to have been regarded by many people in the Midlands as a Biggles of Birmingham."

"I seem to remember a photo from the 1990s of a Brazilian lower-league team with a tree in the middle of their pitch. Can this be confirmed? And are there any other arboreal oddities of note in the wide world of football?"

Rest assured that your memory is not playing tricks on you, for the Brazilian tree of note can be found just outside the centre circle on a pitch at Brás in São Paulo, although this is merely used for leisure, rather than any official matches. More unusual, perhaps, are two other examples of our leafy friends finding their way on to football pitches.

One was planted slap bang in the middle of Chile's national stadium in Santiago by the artist Sebastián Errázuriz during 2006. The project was "a 10-metre high, real magnolia tree planted … where the dictator [General Augusto] Pinochet tortured political prisoners 30 years ago," notes the artist's website. "During a whole week, the decontextualised stadium was open to the public as a park. A cathartic soccer match played before 15,000 people, with the tree in the middle, was the closure of the piece."

Not quite on the playing surface, but occasionally interfering with play was the famous "late tree" at St Albans City's Clarence Park ground, which sat in the middle of terracing behind one of the goals, branching out above the posts and keeper below. When the team finished second in the Premier Division of the Isthmian League in 1993, however, they were denied admittance to the Conference due to a combination of factors. Clarence Park was part of a public park and therefore the oak (and another in the corner of the ground) was protected, while the Conference's ground inspectors also called for £80,000 worth of improvements to upgrade medical facilities, turnstiles and … remove the trees. "The Conference are entitled to make their own rules," said Bernard Tominey, St Albans's chairman at the time. "But what rules are they breaking? Hooligans will climb floodlights more easily than the oaks."

There was one more twist in the tale when, in August 1998, the trees were chopped down after contracting a mystery illness, thus enabling Clarence Park to be renovated in 1999.

"Is it true that a Newcastle United player invented the windscreen wiper?"

Almost, almost. Football can indeed claim for itself a part in the wiper's inception, but it was a Magpies fan, rather than a player, who came up with the idea. In 1908, Gladstone Adams drove his Darracq car from Whitley Bay to Crystal Palace Park for the FA Cup final between Wolves and his beloved Newcastle. Adams's side were the overwhelming favourites against their second division opponents, but the underdogs ran out 3-1 winners and handed Newcastle their third final defeat in four years.

It is fair to suggest then that Adams was not in the best of moods on the journey back up north, and his disposition would have deteriorated further when he soon found himself in the middle of an unseasonable snowstorm. Back then, windscreens had to be cleared by hand and it was during one of these frosty-fingered breaks by the side of the road that Adams came up with the idea of a mechanised blade that could run while the car was in motion. A man of many talents, he would also later become Newcastle United's first official team photographer.

Unfortunately, Adams has a fairly lonely place in the pantheon of football's inventors. Generally, the sport has borrowed concepts from elsewhere. Turnstiles, for instance, were originally used in agriculture as a form of stile, allowing ramblers and farmers to access fields while keeping their sheep and cows herded in. And shin pads, permitted in the FA rules as early as 1874, were also a ripped-off, cut-down version of the cricket pads of the time.

"What with Nigel Clough following in his father Brian's footsteps in becoming the Derby County manager, I was wondering whether any other sons have done likewise?"

Brentford were managed by Bill Dodgin Senior between 1953 and 1957 and his son Bill Dodgin Junior between 1976 and 1980, though nearby Fulham were also double-teamed, as it were, by the Dodgins. Bill Senior took charge of them between 1949 and 1953, while Bill Junior had the job from 1969 to 1972. Fulham seem to go in for this sort of thing, having had their first professional manager, Harry Bradshaw (1904-1909), later succeeded by his son Joe in 1926.

When David Jack (the world's first ever £10,000 signing) managed Southend from 1934 to 1940, he occasionally employed his father Bob – who had bossed the Shrimpers from 1906-1910 to help scout for him, while John Bond (1970-1973) and son Kevin (1988-1992) both held the managerial reins at Bournemouth. And then there is Martin Allen, who became the manager of Cheltenham Town in 2008, where his late father Denis was in charge between 1974 and 1979. "It's special to come back," said Martin, who used to attend games at Whaddon Road as a nipper. "I'm very proud. It's a shame that he's not here. No doubt he will be very proud." Allen subsequently left Cheltenham in 2009.

"What's the longest winless run without a manager getting the sack?"

The "best" that we could uncover belongs to the former Dumbarton manager Jim Fallon, who went on a spectacular 31-game spell in the league without winning a single game between October 1995 and September 1996. Dumbarton actually only managed four draws in that time too, tumbling out of the Scottish first division and then getting off to an inauspicious start in the second.

Dumbarton's sole league victory during Fallon's first season at the helm came at home to Dundee United on 7 October 1995 (1-0), by which point he had already lost his five first games. The Sons, who had actually won their first two games that season before appointing Fallon, went on to post 26 defeats and two draws in their remaining league games. Rather than sack him at this point, the club's board decided to reward Fallon with a new contract. "I feel that it was an unfair playing field for us as we were up against it financially," bemoaned Fallon at the time. "The aim now will be to stabilise the club and make a determined effort to get back up." His team's response was less than impressive. They began the subsequent season with two more draws and a defeat, before the run finally came to an end with a 1-0 away win at Clyde on 7 September 1996.

Alas, Dumbarton still had further to slide yet, and promptly set off on another barren run, drawing one and losing seven of their next eight games before Fallon finally left the club in November. At which point the team promptly won three of their next four, although it could not prevent them spiralling to relegation that season and then to the foot of the third division come the end of the 1997-98 campaign.

"Which clubs have selected an official nickname from some kind of formal poll?"

Sunderland would be the most famous case, having become the "Black Cats" in 2000 after a vote in which more than 11,000 people had their say on the club website. This was a choice soundly in keeping with tradition. According to the club, "the link between Sunderland AFC and the black cat stems originally from a gun battery in 1805 on the River Wear which was renamed the 'Black Cat' battery after the men manning the station heard a mysterious miaow from a wailing black cat. A hundred years later in 1905, a black cat was pictured sitting on a football next to chairman FW Taylor, and three years later a black cat featured on a team photograph."

Elsewhere, fans of Sydney FC were also invited to submit their own suggestions for a new club nickname at the end of 2007. You can draw your own conclusions about the quality of submissions received from the fact they settled for "Sky Blues".

"Have there ever been any instances of a sponsor leaving a club in the lurch with disastrous consequences?"

XL's demise continues to cause West Ham trouble and strife to this day, but the Hammers are far from being alone in having a shirt backer going bust midway through a deal. Take Real Madrid, who lost their sponsor BenQ after the company went bankrupt during the 2006-07 season, barely a year into a five-year deal. Far from being short a euro or two, the Spaniards were able to ride out their troubles and signed a new €60m agreement with gambling company Bwin at the end of the season.

Parma, Cup Winners' Cup champions in 1993, Uefa Cup winners in 1995 and 1999, faced financial ruin in 2003 after the infamous Parmalat scandal broke in Italy. The ruin of the Tanzi family, who owned 98% of the club, led to a player exodus, with the team going from top-half contender to relegation battler, a fight they finally lost in 2007-08.

It is back to England, however, to find a club leading the way in backing the wrong advertising horse. When Charlton Athletic's shirt sponsor all:sports went into administration in September 2005, the unfortunate Addicks soon signed up with Spanish property company Llanera, who proceeded to go bust 2½ years into a 4½-year £6.6m deal.

There is also a case, meanwhile, when a club has been banned from having a particular sponsor's name emblazoned across its players' chests. In 1990, Scarborough's

Black Death Vodka-sponsored shirt (with the additional "Drink in Peace" written below) was banned by the Football League. Amazingly, during a feature on Black Death in 1992, Time magazine noted that "the [US] Bureau of Alcohol, Tobacco and Firearms (ATF), with exquisite literalness, is blocking the liquor on grounds of misleading advertising, since the brand seems to promise poison and plague but delivers only vodka." The ATF's astounding lawsuit was lost and Black Death continues to be distributed to this day.

"My late uncle was a footballer playing for pre-communist China. He always boasted that he played in the 1948 London Olympics. Can you tell me if he did and, if so, how the team got on?"

Good news: your uncle was telling the truth. The Republic of China did send a football team to the Games in 1948 though, sad to relate, their success was limited. They lined up for their first-round match against Turkey on 2 August at the home of football, Green Pond Road, Walthamstow and were sadly eliminated after finishing on the wrong end of a 4-0 walloping. And wearing the No. 5 shirt in that defeat was Man Chi Chau, the man in question.

It would only be fair to note the Chinese team's achievement in simply making the Olympics, what with the nation's government giving next to no funding to its travelling delegation. In order to secure the finances for their trip, the football team embarked on a 32-match tour of Asia, pocketing their share of gate receipts as they went. The party even brought their own food with them, to save on inflated prices in post-war Britain.

The Chinese Olympic team that year featured 33 athletes, all of them male, none of whom made it beyond the preliminary stage of their event. The delegation was then forced to borrow money to make it home. It would be fair to say that state funding for Chinese athletes has somewhat increased in the last 60 years.

"I have a postcard from the Berlin Olympics in 1936 that was sent to an uncle. The sender was Bertie Fulton, an Ulsterman who played for Belfast Celtic, and details a 2-0 win over China. Do you have any further information about him?"

Not only did Fulton start at full-back in Great Britain's first-round win against the Chinese, but he also played and scored in the 5-4 quarter-final defeat against Poland. More information can be found on the Belfast Celtic website, which explains that Fulton, who also played for Larne, "gained all the honours possible in representative matches," and that "he holds a winner's medal for every senior trophy played under the jurisdiction of the IFA."

"Which was the last club to actually carry out the threat: 'We'll let him rot in the reserves'?"

Arguably the most high-profile recent case would be that of Valencia's David Albelda, Santiago Cañizares and Miguel Ángel Angulo. All three had been first-team regulars at the Spanish club, but were dropped by Ronald Koeman soon after he was appointed manager in 2007, then forced to train with the reserves and even banned from team photos and official events.

Speaking in World Soccer magazine, Albelda insisted the club had given no reason for dropping the trio, and yet also refused to sell them. Albelda went on to suggest the decision may have been taken by club president Juan Soler, rather than Koeman. "As we had long contracts and could see that we might be stuck in an uncomfortable position for a long time, I think they hoped that we would get tired of the situation and say 'right, I'm off', breaking our contracts unilaterally," said Albelda, before explaining that they had even taken the club to court over their treatment. "What we did was try to negotiate an exit, but they were never prepared to talk. That was why we ended up in court: it was the only way to force them to sit down and negotiate."

All three players were eventually reinstated at the end of the 2007-08 season – after Koeman was sacked – although Cañizares left the club soon after.

"BATE Borisov's Uefa coefficient was a paltry 1.760 in the 2008-09 season. Has any team ever reached the Champions League group stages, like BATE, with a lower coefficient?"

The answer we received from Uefa's press office was a straightforward "yes", but it should be noted that the system for determining said coefficient has not always been the same. Without drowning you in the minutiae of how these points are earned, let us simply state that each team participating in European competition earns a certain number of Uefa points based on their performance. Since 2004, those teams' coefficients have then been calculated by adding the points they have earned over the previous five years to 33% of their league's coefficient (which is based on the results of all that league's teams in Europe). From 1999 to 2003, the coefficient was worked out in a similar way, except that the team's score was added to 50% of their league's coefficient.

Still with us? It hurts our head just to write this. Before 1999, however, the calculations were completely different. Although the last five years' results were counted then too, a far lower number of points were awarded per season and the league coefficient was not included. In 1998, for instance, the top team was Paris St Germain with 8.716. In 2008-09, Chelsea led the way with 124.996.

With all that in mind, we can tell you that BATE's coefficient is comfortably the lowest since 2004, beating previous record-holders FC Artmedia Bratislava, who thumped Celtic on the way to reaching the group stage with a coefficient of 4.850 in 2005-06.

"Given the banter and time spent among themselves at football clubs, I was wondering if there are any random examples of player forfeits among themselves?"

For some strange, Only Fools and Horses-inspired reason, Robin Reliants feature in at least two cases. Firstly, the Leeds United squad got their hands on a yellow three-wheeler, which would be forced upon the player voted to have performed worst in training during any given week back in 2001. Jonathan Woodgate was the initial recipient of the £1,500 motor − which the squad had funded themselves − and was forced to leave his far more plush mode of transport in the club car park for the seven-day period. "I thought it was Trotters Independent Traders turning up," chuckled then-chairman Peter Ridsdale. According to Observer Sport Monthly, however, "the car − which was due to be signed by the squad and auctioned off at the end of the season − was smashed up by vandals. 'It is appalling people can commit a crime like this,' fumed manager David O'Leary."

In 2008, Portsmouth's players rustled up a similar plan and chipped in to buy a bright blue Reliant, which soon had one careful owner in the shape of David James. "It gave us all an added incentive to perform well in training," claimed James. Then again, when team-mate Sean Davis was handed the keys later that year, he drove it back to the club's Eastleigh training ground in a newly-pimped-out A-Team paint job, the theme tune blaring out of its speakers.

Managers also like to get in on the forfeit act, and it probably won't come as much of a shock to learn that Neil Warnock and Ian Holloway are among their number. In an interview with the Independent in 2009, Warnock revealed what happened after one particular training session during a snowy February. "At the end, the winning team picked two members of the losing side," he explained. "They had to stand on the goal-line, minus certain items of clothing, while the rest of the lads had three snowballs to throw at them from 12 yards. If our strikers could hit the target in matches as well as they did with their snowballs, we'd have won promotion already."

Rather less severe was Holloway's 2006 method of making his underperforming Plymouth players sport a "Joey Barton bottom" – apparently a pair of shorts with a plastic backside attached to them – in tribute to Barton's mooning of Everton fans that year. "If a player's nominated, he'll wear it, no problem," said Holloway. "It was supposed to be for the worst player, but it can be awarded for anything. One time, one of them couldn't go out because his girlfriend wouldn't let him and he was picked. It's been brilliant."

Stretching the question to different sports, we even received an email from the former Hull FC rugby league player Craig Farrell, who recalled one rule from during his spell at the club. "If you played first-team rugby at any point during the season – regardless of how long you were on the pitch – and didn't score, you had to perform a 'nudie' at the end of the year," he wrote. "A 'nudie' was one full lap around the training pitch wearing nothing but your boots and socks (on your feet). At the time I was 18 and playing for the reserves when the first team was ravaged by injury, and was duly called up to make a couple of substitute appearances in 56-4 and 54-4 defeats to the Bradford Bulls and Wigan Warriors, respectively. Needless to say, you could've seen me trotting around the old Boulevard in only my boots and socks a couple of months later."

"Who was the last player to score for England sporting a proper moustache? I think it was Viv Anderson, but a friend is convinced it was Kenny Sansom."

Well, if there's money riding on it, you're the one in profit. Sansom's only goal for England came against Finland in October 1984 during a World Cup qualifier, while Anderson scored his second and final England goal against Yugoslavia in November 1986. The two are in fact split by another moustachioed scorer, Danny Wallace, who found the net in January 1986. More recently, David Beckham, Darius Vassell and Ledley King have hit the target for

England while showing off some facial furniture, but theirs are more beard-'tache combos, and certainly not what you would call "a proper moustache".

"According to my reckoning, St Petersburg used to be the biggest city in Europe to have never had one of its clubs in the Champions League group stages. Now that Zenit have achieved this, which city holds the mantle? Is it Budapest?"

Well, your reckoning is half right. St Petersburg was the largest city never to make the Champions League groups, but Budapest (the 10th largest city in Europe) is not the new holder of the title and, frankly, we're a little disappointed you managed to forget Ferencvaros's ground-breaking campaign of 1995-96. Instead, the Belarussian capital of Minsk (12th largest with a population of 1,677,000) takes the crown.

Of course, European football history does not begin and end with the creation of group stages in 1991, so which city is the largest to have never qualified for the European Cup proper? Minsk quickly counts itself out; Dinamo, of course, were old regulars and even made the last eight in 1983-84. The next likely lads, Warsaw (13th), also has a history richer than its current status – Legia made the semis in 1970. Belgrade (14th) won the ruddy thing with Red Star in 1991, so instead we must look to the Ukrainian metropolis of Kharkiv, Europe's 16th biggest city, the 1,494,000 population of which are yet to watch the continent's premier club competition come to town.

"International tournaments always stagger their knock-out rounds, understandably, but is there any evidence to suggest that the teams qualifying from the earlier semi-final have an advantage in the final?"

Firstly, a minor question correction. The staggered semi is a relatively recent addition to the European Championships and the World Cup, and it has not really caught on at all in Africa or Asia. Before Euro 76 and Italia 90, semi-finals were played on the same day (if at all), with the solitary exception of the 1966 World Cup.

The statistics also suggest no particular benefit for teams with an extra day's rest. Of the eight European Championships to feature staggered semis (1980 is technically an exception, but Belgium played their final group game a day later than West Germany, their opponents in the final, so we'll count it), four have been won by teams benefiting from an extra day's rest (France in 2000, Holland in 1988, France in 1984 and Czechoslovakia in 1976), and five have been won by those playing in the later game.

Prior to the 2010 World Cup finals, there have been five tournaments with staggered last-four matches, with only one – Italy in 2006 – being won by the team who played the first.

In South America, it is five Copa América wins to three in favour of the teams playing their semi-final a day later, while in the Asian Nations Cup, it's two against one the other way (semis have been played on the same day since 1992). Concacaf's Gold Cup, meanwhile, has been a graveyard for those with an extra day's preparation before the final: on all five occasions – 2003, 2000, 1998, 1996 and 1993 – when the semis have been played on different days, the team playing earliest lost.

Finally, the Africa Cup of Nations semi-finals have been staged on the same day since 1963. This may or may not have something to do with the fact that, back in 1962, Ethiopia used their extra four days' downtime to thump Egypt 4-2 in the final.

"Barcelona have teams playing handball and basketball, in addition to football, while Panathinaikos and CSKA Moscow also spring to mind as competing in a vast array of disicplines. Which club has won titles in the most different sports and which has the most titles overall?"

Europe is teeming with clubs that participate in all manner of sporting disciplines. SS Lazio is probably the one that spreads itself the widest, with teams competing in more than 37 different sports from cricket to parachute jumping.

In 1987, the awards dinner at Turkish club Galatasaray must have been quite a bash as they won titles in 16 different sports, including wheelchair basketball, rowing, sailing, judo and motor sports. AS Roma, Porto, Olympiakos, Hamburg and Benfica are all other multi-tasking sporting titans, but the biggest "Sport Billy" of the lot has to be FC Barcelona, who boast professional teams in football, basketball, handball, futsal and roller hockey. Amateur teams also represent Barça in hockey, athletics, baseball, cycling, field hockey, figure skating and volleyball. And, to answer the question, we reckon that their 2009-10 Fifa Club World Cup success was Barcelona's 384th title, according to their club records. That mantelpiece must need some serious reinforcing.

"Have any teams ever won the FA Cup without conceding a goal?"

As well as wreaking havoc with our asthma, our trawl through the Cup's dusty annals has thrown up three teams who claimed glory without being beaten once at the back. First came The Wanderers, who achieved the feat on their way to lifting the second-ever FA Cup in March 1873. Then again, they only had to play one game: as holders of the trophy – they had beaten Royal Engineers in the inaugural final – Wanderers received a bye straight to the showpiece, where they faced Oxford University at Lillie Bridge. A crowd of around 3,000 watched Edward Bowen keep a clean sheet, helping the Battersea-based club to a 2-0 win and the second of what turned out to be five FA Cup triumphs in the 1870s.

Sixteen seasons later, in 1888-89, Preston North End breezed past Bootle, Grimsby Town, Birmingham St George's and West Brom without conceding on their way to the final, before hammering Wolves 3-0 when they got there. Bury were equally impregnable as they beat Wolves, Sheffield United, Notts County, Aston Villa and Derby (who they battered 6-0 in the final) in 1902-03.

"Who were Wanderers, and what happened to them?"

Founded 13 years prior to their first FA Cup triumph in 1872 as Forest Football Club, based in Leytonstone, east London, Wanderers were an amateur outfit comprised chiefly of former public schoolboys and became one of the Football Association's original members in 1863. A year later, they upped sticks and wandered across town to Battersea Park and adopted Wanderers as their name. Their captain Charles Alcock was, handily, also the chairman of the FA between 1870 and 1895, and it was he, on 20 July 1871, who decided: "It is desirable that a Challenge Cup should be played." (Alcock, educated at Harrow, also played cricket for Middlesex, and is viewed by many as the "inventor" of the FA Cup, international football and Test cricket).

In the first FA Cup final, held at the Kennington Oval in March 1872, Wanderers beat Royal Engineers 1-0 courtesy of a goal from AH Chequer (a pseudonym for Morton Peto Betts, who had been cup-tied having initially represented Harrow Chequers in the competition). After notching up another four wins in the competition, Wanderers eventually dissolved in 1887 once the likes of Old Carthusians and Old Etonians schools had established their own clubs. Writing in The English Illustrated Magazine in 1891, Alcock claimed that "the success of the Wanderers is so closely identified with the success of Association Football in its earlier days that it is impossible to dissever the club from any attempt to follow closely the various stages which have marked the growth of the game".

"A friend of mine was telling me about an Icelandic referee who disallowed a goal because his teeth had fallen out. Am I right to assume he was talking bobbins?"

Technically you would be right to assume that, but only because the gummy official in question was actually Danish. Henning Erikstrup had been preparing to whistle for full-time in Noerager's 4-3 win against Ebeltoft when his false teeth tumbled out of his mouth and on to the pitch. Ebeltoft equalised moments later only for Erikstrup, who had not seen the goal, to immediately rule it out on the grounds that he would have whistled before it went in.

"I had to get my teeth back before some player put his

big foot on them," parped the referee afterwards when asked why he didn't just whistle without his teeth in.

"The memorable 1961 British Home Championship yielded an astonishing 40 goals from its six matches. Has another tournament ever bettered this goal ratio (6.66 per game)?"

It has indeed, more often than not at the South Pacific Games, which have long provided a rich goal-scoring seam. In 1963, when the event was first held in Suva, Fiji, 49 goals were scored over six matches, an average of 8.17 per match. This whopping tally owed much to Tahiti's 18-0 victory over the Solomon Islands in the bronze-medal match.

The net bulged even more frequently at the 1971 tournament, staged in Tahiti. The hosts' 30-0 Group A win over the Cook Islands, themselves also on the wrong end of a 16-1 drubbing by Papua New Guinea and a 15-1 defeat to Fiji, set the tone for a competition in which 103 goals were scored in 10 games: an average of 10.3 per match.

Even this can be topped by the 109 goals scored in Oceania Group One qualifying for the 2002 World Cup, when an average of 10.9 were scored in every game. And mention must also go to the 2006 Viva World Cup, the bi-annual competition organised by the Nouvelle Fédération-Board for teams unaffiliated to Fifa, produced 57 goals in six matches – an average of 9.5 per game.

"Why is a derby match so-called? And who do Derby play in their derby?"

Derby County haven't had a derby in the truest sense of the word to look forward to for more than 115 years, having merged with the city's only other major side, Derby Midland, in 1891. Then again, try telling any Rams fans that their matches with bitter rivals Nottingham Forest, who sit barely 15 miles away across the A52 (or the Brian Clough Way as it is also known), don't count.

As far as the word "derby" goes, we'll hand over to word origin expert Michael Quinlon, who explains on his excellent World Wide Words website how the term derived from the horse race known as the Derby Stakes. "First run in 1780, it was named after Edward Stanley, 12th Earl of Derby," he begins. "It soon became established as the high point of the racing season as part of the meeting at Epsom in Surrey in early June. It became so important that other classic races were named after it, such as the Kentucky Derby.

"Derby day, the day of the race, became a hugely popular event, not just for the toffs but as a big day out for all Londoners, a public holiday in all but name. Great numbers of people drove or took the train down to Epsom, making a day of it with picnics and lots to drink. In 1906, [the journalist] George R. Sims wrote: 'With the arrival of Derby Day we have touched the greatest day of all in London; it may almost be said to be the Londoners' greatest holiday – their outing or saturnalia.'

"At about the time George Sims was writing, the word moved into more general use to describe any highly popular and well-attended event. In particular, it came to be applied to a fixture between two local sides, first called a local Derby and then abbreviated (in Britain we've tended to keep the full form, to avoid confusion with the Derby itself)."

"While watching Wales take on Russia in 2003, I noticed that the score in the top left corner of the television screen was WAL 0 1 RUS. Removing the numbers, can any other teams (international or otherwise) make up the name of an aquatic mammal?"

Where to start with such a question? Well, the imagined meeting of Belgium and Uganda would produce BELUGA, a species of white whale and also a type of sturgeon, but beyond this we could only add Turkey v Botswana (TURBOT). Moving randomly to a club football example, we are obviously far too mature to find any humour in the Arsenal de Sarandi v Newell's Old Boys match from Argentina, which produced the TV match status of ARS v NOB. Obviously.

"Is there any truth in the tale that Harry Redknapp once fielded a spectator during a West Ham game?"

Incredibly, the legend appears to be true. In 1998, Redknapp's Hammers side were playing Oxford City in a pre-season friendly when ... well, we'll let Harry take up the tale:

"Lee Chapman was playing for us at the time," recounted Redknapp in the Sun. "All through the first half, some tattooed skinhead behind me was giving Lee terrible stick. At half-time I turned to this bloke who had 'West Ham' etched on his neck and asked: 'Can you play as good as you talk?' He looked totally confused. So I told him he was going to get his dream to play for West Ham. We sent him down the tunnel and he reappeared 10 minutes later all done out in the strip. He ran out on to the pitch and a journalist from the local Oxford paper sidled up and asked 'Who's that Harry?' I said 'What? Haven't you been watching the World Cup? That's the great Bulgarian!' Tittyshev I called him! 'Er, oh yeah,' the guy replied and wrote the name down in his notepad. The fella wasn't bad – actually, he scored!"

"Having read about dogs running on to the field of play, I wondered if any of our canine friends have actually scored a goal in doing so?"

Newcastle Town had good right to go barking mad in November 1985 during a Staffordshire Sunday Cup tie against Stoke-based team Knave of Clubs. "We were losing 2-0," recalled the Knave of Clubs secretary, David Hall. "One of our players was running down the field with only the goalkeeper to beat. He tried a shot from 15 yards out and miscued it, so it was going well wide. The dog ran on to the field, jumped up at the ball and headed it. The ball flew into the net." To Newcastle's chagrin, the referee let the goal stand due to there being no FA rule about canine intervention.

Meanwhile, a seagull even got its name on the scoresheet in 1999 during Stalybridge Celtic Colts' game against Hollingworth Juniors in Manchester. With the Colts 2-1 up, their striker Danny Worthington's long-range volley was apparently heading over when it struck the swooping bird and deflected into the net. "The next thing I knew everyone was cheering so I put my arms in the air and started cheering," Reuters quoted the 13-year-old as saying. "It was then I realised the seagull had scored the goal." Briefly stunned, the seagull recovered and soared off into the distance, unaware of the role it played in condemning poor Hollingworth to a 7-1 defeat.

"Cochabamba's Club Jorge Wilstermann is named after Bolivia's first commercial pilot. Are there any other teams out there named after individuals?"

There are dozens of men (and several women) who have the privilege of a club named in their honour. Discounting those named after saints (because there are so many of them), they include:

Vasco da Gama: Formed out of a rowing club already named after the famous Portuguese explorer.

Willem II: The Eredivisie side from Tilburg were renamed after King Willem II of the Netherlands from the original Tilburgia. Tilburg housed his military headquarters.

Newell's Old Boys: Isaac Newell came into the world in Strood, Kent, on 24 April 1853. By the time he left it, on 16 October 1907, he had helped create what would go on to be one of Argentinian football's most famous clubs.

Vélez Sársfield: In 1909, torrential rain brought an end to a kick about in a field near Vélez Sársfield station – now Floresta station – in Buenos Aires. Three men (Julio Guglielmone, Martin Potillo and Nicolas Martín Moreno), soaked to the skin, took refuge in a nearby railway tunnel and were soon lose in reverie about proper pitches to play on, with proper kit to play in. And so, on New Year's Day 1910, a lovely new club was founded, named after the place of its spiritual birth. The station (and therefore the club) was named after a famous Argentinian judge called Dalmacio Vélez Sársfield (1801-1875). Sársfield, who reformed Argentina's constitution and its civil code, was actually descended from Irish immigrants who were employed in the military in Argentina during the mid-18th century.

Club Atlético Aldovisi: Another team from Argentina, whose name originates from the first two letters of the last names of its four original founders: Allard, Dollfus, Sillard and Wiriott – the W changed to a V due to there being no W key on the telegraph that originally announced the club's inception.

Club Deportivo O'Higgins: Born in Chile, Bernardo O'Higgins Riquelme was the illegitimate son of Ambrosio O'Higgins, a future governor of Chile and viceroy of Peru, himself born to Spanish parents in Sligo, Ireland. He grew up to become a leader of the home side in the Chilean War of Independence and is viewed as one of the country's founding fathers. When two clubs in the city of Rancagua merged in 1955, they kept the prefix of one of the clubs, O'Higgins Braden.

Club Presidente Hayes: One of the few (only?) clubs named after a US president. Rutherford B. Hayes showed great compassion towards Paraguay after taking charge of peace talks following the War of the Triple Alliance (which sounds like it should be in Star Wars, but was actually an exceptionally bloody affair in the 1860s involving Paraguay, Argentina, Uruguay and Brazil). Hayes's role led to a number of institutions (and a city, Villa Hayes) being named in his honour, including this football club from Asunción.

Club Deportivo Luis Ángel Firpo: The oldest club in El Salvador, it was originally named Tecún Umán but changed in honour of the Argentinian boxer's epic bout and narrow defeat to the heavyweight champion Jack Dempsey in 1923.

Renato Curi Angolana: The Serie D outfit are an amalgamation of two clubs: dell'Angolana and Renato Curi, the latter of which was created in memory of a midfielder who played for Perugia in the 1970s and helped them get promoted to Serie A. He tragically died of a heart attack on the pitch during a match against Juventus in October 1977 aged just 24. Perugia's stadium is also named in his honour.

Club Atlético Douglas Haig: Why would a club from Pergamino, just north of Buenos Aires, name itself after a British first world war Field Marshall? According to the club: "On 18 November 1918 after the resounding victory of the Allied forces, a group of British workers on the Argentinian central railroad decided to start a club to participate in the local soccer championship. This required the consent and support of the chief of the railway, Ronald

Leslie, who, as a condition, requested that the club take the name of General Douglas Haig."

Club Deportivo Cruz Antonio Tomba: Named after not just one, but two individuals, they are the result of a 1930 compromise when Sportivo Godoy Cruz (named after a signatory of the 1816 Argentinian Declaration of Independence, Tomás Godoy Cruz) merged with Deportivo Bodega Antonio Tomba (Tomba's store was a club sponsor).

Colo-Colo: The only Chilean side to have won the Copa Libertadores were named after Colocolo, a Mapuche chief of the 16th century. The name translates as 'mountain cat'.

Deportivo Walter Ferretti: According to a 1988 Washington Post article, Ferretti was "one of the Sandanistas' outstanding revolutionaries" in Nicaragua, who "led a crack counter-insurgency unit against the US-backed contra rebels". Following his death in a 1988 road accident, the old Ministry of the Interior team was subsequently renamed from MINT in his memory.

Wingate and Finchley: The Ryman League Division One North outfit owe the "Wingate" part of their name to General Orde Charles Wingate, who oversaw the inception of the Israeli Army during the Second World War. In a bid to battle anti-Semitism, a group of English Jews set up a club in 1946 and named it in his honour, before a merger with Finchley FC in 1991.

Marconi Stallions: Currently in the New South Wales Premier League, the Stallions are named after the inventor of the wireless, Guglielmo Marconi. "Marconi was chosen because of its appeal to both Italians and Australians," explains the club's website. "His scientific genius provided a connection in the form of communication between different cultures."

Jomo Cosmos: After returning from a spell playing for the New York Cosmos, Jomo Sono bought South African side Highlands Park and renamed them after himself. He later managed the national team and is currently head coach of the Cosmos.

Kallon FC: Formerly known as Sierra Fisheries, the Sierra Leone club was bought out and renamed by the much-travelled former Inter striker Mohamed Kallon for $30,000 in 2002. As owner, chairman and player at the club, Kallon told the BBC in December 2009 that he viewed himself "as a role model in Sierra Leone football and I believe I'll achieve my objective ... and help the local game grow".

Joe Public FC: Formed in 1996, the Trinidad and Tobago club, once home to Kenwyne Jones and the former Dundee and Gillingham defender Brent Sancho, is named after, well, everybody.

"While many clubs maintain the rather lame tradition of reserving their No. 12 for their fans, I noticed that Oldham choose the No. 40 instead. Do any other clubs reserve different numbers for supporters?"

They do indeed, among them Stockport County, who listed the darts player Tony "Silverback" O'Shea on the back page of their matchday programme each week as No. 180, on account of him reaching the 2009 BDO World Championship final. "Tony is a big friend of the club," said Des Hinks, the club's media manager. "We are all extremely proud of him getting to the darts final, and I know the town of Stockport is as well. Tony is always promoting the club because he wears our colours wherever he is competing. So we thought it would be nice to pay our own tribute to him."

Returning to the question, Oldham's No. 40 shirt is given over to "The Spirit of Oldham". "This is in recognition of the wonderful support given by fans over what was a very difficult period for the club during the summer of 2003," explained the club, referring to the departure of chairman Chris Moore and subsequent entering of administration at Boundary Park. Down at Bournemouth, meanwhile, the fans get No. 32, while the North Stand at their Fitness First Stadium even has the No. 27.

In Greece, Panathinaikos reserve the No. 13 for their Ultras, who congregate around Gate 13, while Swedish side Djurgårdens IF rather oddly keep No. 1 for their supporters.

"Why do Israeli clubs – and the national team – play in European competitions? Surely they should be knocking about with Asian teams: their neighbours Syria, Jordan and Lebanon do."

You may have noticed that, unlike that Australian soap opera theme tune, neighbours do not always become good friends. Don't take it from us, though, here's Uefa's statement on the matter: "According to Uefa statutes, in exceptional circumstances, a national football association that is situated in another continent may be admitted for membership, provided that it is not a member of the confederation of that continent, or of any other confederation, and that Fifa approves its membership of Uefa.

"Due to the tense political situation in this particular part of the world in the beginning of the 1990s, Israel asked for its affiliation to Uefa. Its clubs were not given the chance to participate in club competitions under the umbrella of the Asian Football Confederation as most of the Arab countries objected to meeting Israeli teams. In an effort to contribute to the development of football and to give an opportunity to as many people as possible to enjoy the game, the Uefa executive committee decided to accept the affiliation request." This took place in three steps: the admission of Israeli teams into European club competitions in September 1991; the "provisory" admission of the Football Association of Israel (IFA) to Uefa in 1993; and the IFA's "definite" admission to Uefa on 28 April 1994.

In a slightly different vein, there were the subsequent "exceptional circumstances" of Kazakhstan's 2002 admission to Uefa, despite bordering China, Kyrgystan, Turkmenistan and Uzbekistan, after resigning from the Asian Football Confederation. "In that sense, [they] were homeless," explained Mike Lee, Uefa's communications director at the time. "They believe that they're more naturally European, they want to be more European-turning in their outlook as a nation and as an economy. If a country has a historical and territorial base that is relevant it has a right to pursue that." An understandably delighted Kazakhstan FA president Rakhat Aliyev added: "Practically speaking, it means more contacts with Europe and more investment projects. It will also lead to a better future for players and especially young people in the country. It will lead to a higher professional level."

"In betting terms, what is the shortest pre-kick-off price to have ever been offered for a game to be drawn?"

"The only time we offer odds-on draws are at the end of the season in the Italian league," explained Graham Sharpe, of bookmakers William Hill. "It happens every season – two teams need a draw, and it ends in a draw."

The shortest price that Betfred have ever put up on a game to finish all square reveals the continuing of a trend. "It would have been right at the end of the 2006-07

Italian league season," suggested the company's John Wilde. "Torino and Livorno began at 4-5 for a draw and got backed in to 2-5." Why was everyone so certain, you doubtless ask? "Both teams only needed a point to avoid relegation." Funnily enough, the game ended 0-0.

Simon Clare, of Coral, agreed that Italian games can sometimes have a whiff of stalemate around them, and suggested that the bookies may have seen this particular game coming. However, the shortest odds on a draw that he could remember occurred during the final match day of the 2006-07 Champions League group stages, when Arsenal and FC Porto played out a mutually acceptable nil-niller after being priced at 4-5 to draw. "Conspiracy theories will come up, but the likelihood with these games is that the teams will end up playing it safe," explained Clare.

"Which was the last team to win the English top flight playing in a striped home kit?"

The answer depends on how discerning you are about your stripes. Obviously, we're not going to count teams with a few skinny lines down their sleeves and shorts, nor indeed will we accept Blackburn's half-and-half blue and white blocks, but would you accept the alternating shades of red on Arsenal's title-winning top from 1988-89?

If not, then the white pinstripes Liverpool sported during their triumphant 1983-84 campaign are a little more clear cut. But if you will only settle for wholehearted, chunky, even slices of markedly different colour, then you actually have to go all the way back to 1935-36, when Sunderland won the old first division in their traditional red and white.

"What is the longest stretch that Manchester United have gone without winning a Premier League game?"

In the competition's inaugural 1992-93 season, United went seven games without collecting maximum points in a league match. During a particularly goal-shy period – they scored just six times in a 12-game run in all competitions as Mark Hughes and Brian McClair searched feverishly for a back door – United drew five and lost two between 19 September and 21 November before they eventually trounced Oldham 3-0.

A few days later, Alex Ferguson signed Eric Cantona and the rest is history. United finished the season with 84 points and won their first league championship in 26 years, beating their nearest rivals Aston Villa by 10 points. Since then, Ferguson's men did lose five Premier League games in seven during their winter of discontent in 2001, but then again, they have – at the time of writing – won 10 further top-flight titles since that 92-93 breakthrough.

"Did the great and the good of football officialdom (OK, Sepp Blatter) ever play the game professionally?"

Not to such a standard, no, but you may be thrilled to know that football's biggest cheese did play as a striker at an amateur level for a number of years in Switzerland. Indeed, according to Fifa's official website, Blatter's career spanned a whopping 23 years from 1948 (this is presumably including youth football, as he would have been 12 at the time) to 1971, most if not all of which was spent with his hometown side FC Visp.

"I scored a lot of goals," boasted Blatter to interviewers from CNN as they filmed a 2006 documentary about him. "That's not a false modesty – it's really true, especially at the youth level." We would be inclined not to believe him about this, or the story about splitting a pair of boots with a friend ("I took the left, he took the right") for his first ever game, but since he did own up to diving ("I was not a perfect player") and having a go at referees during his playing days in the very same interview, we're prepared to give him the benefit of the doubt.

"In 1988, my team KV Mechelen played European football for the first time and they won the Cup Winners' Cup. Has any other team won a major European competition in their first ever season in Europe (apart from in the first season of continental competition, obviously)?"

They have, though how many others depends somewhat on the definition of "major European tournament". In total, four other teams have gone all the way on their first forays into Europe, but three of them did so in the Fairs Cup. Barcelona (1958), Valencia (1962) and Newcastle (1969) are the trio in question, though even then Barça's triumph might not quite meet the criteria: they didn't actually lift the trophy until 1958, an impressive three years after their inaugural Fairs Cup campaign kicked off in 1955-56. West Ham, on the other hand, matched Mechelen's feat exactly, having won the Cup Winners' Cup in 1965 at their first attempt in Europe.

We should also point out that by counting the Fairs Cup, we are also excluding some teams from our list. Nottingham Forest, for instance, had played in two Fairs Cups (1961-62 and 1967-68), but no other main European tournaments when they won the European Cup in 1979.

"What is the youngest ever line-up to feature in the Premier League?"

On 7 May 2006, Middlesbrough warmed up for their Uefa Cup final hammering at the hands of Sevilla by resting the majority of their squad for the trip to Fulham. Goalkeeper Ross Turnbull (20) and defenders Andrew Davies (20), Matthew Bates (18), David Wheater (18) and Andrew Taylor (18) featured in a back-line boasting a remarkable average age of 18.8.

Steve McClaren's side that day contained seven teenagers at an average age of just 20, with one player – the veteran 26-year-old Malcolm Christie – over the age of 21. "It's a proud day for Middlesbrough," declared McClaren after the game, which they lost 1-0 to an 85th-minute Heidar Helguson penalty, "and for Steve Gibson, the chairman, who always wanted as his dream to field a team of players born within 30 miles of [our] stadium. Fifteen of the 16 in the squad were that. The performance was heroic."

"A friend told me that in the mid-70s, the new victors were displaying their recently-won FA Cup at pitchside during a match, only for an opposition player to kick the ball, full-bloodedly, at the trophy and knock it flying. Is this true?"

The match in question featured Sunderland and QPR, and the incident, at least according to the man in question's autobiography, was notorious Hoops midfielder Stan Bowles. The teams met in the old division two on 9 May 1973, only four days after Sunderland had won the FA Cup, and the club decided to parade the trophy around their ground, then Roker Park. After the parade, the cup was placed on a table at the side of the pitch before … well, let's hear it straight from the horse's mouth.

"There were a couple of us who had a bet on who could knock it off the table with the ball first," recalled Bowles. "With the ball at my feet, I tear off straight across the park. Everyone on the pitch is just staring at me – and then, bang! The FA Cup goes shooting up in the air. The whole ground knew that I'd done it on purpose – then the Sunderland fans go ape. They want my balls in their sandwiches. I wound up their fans even more by scoring a couple of goals and, in the end, there was a pitch invasion. At least I got my tenner, and my picture on News at Ten. And all because I was just having a bit of a laugh."

However, the then-QPR manager Gordon Jago, subsequently got back in touch with a different view of events that day: "The truth is that yes, the FA Cup was knocked off the table during the game against Sunderland, but not by Stan Bowles. It was Tony Hazell, the QPR defender. At some time during the game, Tony cleared a ball and it knocked the cup flying. This incident really upset the home fans; so much so that the referee took both teams from the field to let tempers cool. The game was eventually restarted and we finished 3-0 winners. Stan had someone write a book for him and he tells the story about a bet and that he deliberately knocked the cup off the table. Fiction! I do not know if Tony or any of the other players have contacted Stan to correct him, but that story is typical of him and no doubt it helped to sell the book."

"Who has scored for Newcastle United and also saved a penalty for Manchester United?"

Hmm, sounds like a trick question to us. How about … the Honey Monster? The big yellow beast once scored a last-minute FA Cup final winner for the Magpies in a Sugar Puffs advert made during the Kevin Keegan era ("I just had to get the big man off the bench," says Keegan). Incredibly, the multi-talented beast donned Peter Schmeichel's gloves in a later commercial, holding his nerve to make a flying penalty save for Manchester United.

As a result of that initial advert, sales of Sugar Puffs in the north-east fell by up to 20% after rival Sunderland fans boycotted the cereal, much as they have with Northern Rock and a host of other products and services linked to the Tyneside club down the years. But then, in 2009, the advertising men at Frank PR, on behalf of Honey Monster Foods, released another advert, this time showing the big yellow machine working out in a gym … wearing a Sunderland shirt. "Honey Monster didn't expect the reaction that came after his advert with Kevin Keegan," Frank PR's Ben Jun-Tai told the Sunday Sun. "By wearing his Sunderland shirt in his workout video, he just wanted to show that he wasn't taking sides. Honey Monster does not support any one team, he just loves football."

"I seem to remember the Peruvian goalkeeper at the 1978 World Cup finals getting booked for a foul in the opponents' half of the field. Is my brain playing tricks on me?"

Your memory served you well, for the random player in question was Ramón *"El Loco"* Quiroga, who picked up a yellow card for fouling Grzegorz Lato in Poland's half during the Poles' 1-0 second-round group win. It was the second time that Quiroga had been caught in Poland's half during the game, but on this occasion, Lato received the ball on the left and turned only to find the goalkeeper in his face. After the foul, Quiroga retreated, head bowed and hands behind his back in contrition, as the referee showed him the yellow card. On the video highlights of the game, laughter can be heard ringing out from the pundits during *El Loco*'s advances, with the commentator noting: "The crowd don't mind the yellow card. They quite like being part of the occasion."

"After reading about the referee Mike Reed celebrating a goal at Anfield, have there been other instances of inappropriate officiating conduct?"

At the end of the 1971 FA Cup final, Norman Burtenshaw was caught on film falling to his knees and pumping his fists towards the heavens after Arsenal's 2-1 extra-time win over Liverpool, though the referee himself later claimed he was simply celebrating the fact the game had not gone to a replay. Controversy would dog Burtenshaw during his 11-year career (a day after the Football League introduced a new disciplinary clampdown, Burtenshaw dismissed George Best for calling him "a fucking disgrace") and only a few months after the Wembley game, he presided over Arsenal's 6-2 battering of Benfica. So incensed by his performance, Rothman's Football Yearbook 1972-73 notes that "the Portuguese players attack referee Burtenshaw, who in turn reports the entire team to Uefa".

Burtenshaw had already had a chance to brush up on his self-defence skills a few years earlier, mind. When Aston Villa beat Millwall 2-1 in October 1967, the Den crowd were so angered that they stormed the pitch and surrounded the referee. He had to be carried from the pitch after being knocked unconscious.

The German official Wolf-Dieter Ahlenfelder, by contrast,

was knocked sideways by several pre-match liveners. During Werder Bremen's November 1975 Bundesliga match against Hannover 96, referee Ahlenfelder surprised everyone with a series of unusual decisions, chief among them blowing for half-time after just 29 minutes. After a linesman notified Ahlenfelder of his mistake, he played 16 minutes of added time. When the half-time interval was correctly reached, Ahlenfelder then stuck his tongue out at a photographer. "For this show we could have charged a higher entrance fee," sniffed the Werder president Franz Böhmert after the 0-0 draw. Ahlenfelder, of course, denied drinking alcohol at the time, but later he admitted having partaken in "several Maltesers" (schnapps) before the game. And to make things really clear to the layman, he declared: "We are men – we don't drink Fanta."

"What is the furthest a national side has gone in the World Cup finals without conceding a goal?"

While the competition's format hasn't always been the same, the host nation from 1990 can still claim to have lasted the longest without having to pick the ball out of their net. Italy, with Walter Zenga between the posts, managed to reach the semi-finals after going 517 minutes without conceding. Sadly for them, when Claudio Caniggia finally breached their defences, his goal took the game with Argentina to penalties, a shoot-out the Italians would lose 4-3.

"Who is/are the most foolish football fan/s ever? Perhaps someone spending an obscene amount of money on a ticket, only to watch them lose, or a bunch of supporters celebrating that little bit too soon?"

The prize for premature celebration can only go to the fans of one team, Schalke 04, who mistakenly thought their team had won the Bundesliga title on the final day of the 2000-01 season. But hadn't. Needing to win at their Parkstadion against Unterhaching and hope Hamburg could upset Bayern Munich at home, Schalke fought back from behind on two occasions to win 5-3. Then came the news their fans had been waiting for: Hamburg had taken a 90th-minute lead, prompting Schalke supporters to celebrate what they felt simply had to be a first league championship since 1958. As the fans poured on to the pitch, in Munich Bayern launched one final injury-time attack. After winning an indirect free-kick inside the Hamburg penalty area, Stefan Effenberg tapped the ball to Patrik Andersson, who drilled home the title-winning goal. Cue red faces and broken hearts back in a disbelieving Gelsenkirchen.

Moving swiftly on, the Newcastle supporter Robert Nesbitt suffered an even more painful experience – physically, at least – in 1995 when he chose to have a large image of Andy Cole in full Magpies garb tattooed on his right thigh ... two days before Cole left for Manchester United. Likewise, the Manchester City fan Chris Atkinson got a little too excited when Garry Cook launched his ill-fated trip to Milan in a bid to sign Kaká and got the Brazilian's name inscribed on his chest, only for the deal to fall through and the player to join Real Madrid instead. "I couldn't believe it and rushed out to check all the news channels," a disconsolate Atkinson told the Manchester Evening News. "I got carried away by the emotion of him coming here." Unfortunately, Atkinson didn't learn his lesson and was soon regretting having the legend "Robinho" tattooed just above his Kaká one. "I can't believe this has happened again," he said. "I'm gutted."

The advent of betting exchanges has created even more fatuous fans, believing they can make a quick buck by placing huge wagers at short-priced odds. Take the case of the Tottenham supporter who fell foul of his team's miserable recent home record against Manchester United and found his way to No. 5 in totalgambler.com's list of "most outrageous gambles". "It's 29 September 2001 and half-time at White Hart Lane," it recalls. "Spurs are leading 3-0 and, in a bid to impress his girlfriend, one Tottenham fan stakes his entire mortgage on Spurs to win the game. United go on to win 5-3 and the punter goes home to an empty house (and an empty bed)."

However, the most stupid football supporters in history must surely come from this National Criminal Intelligence Service (NCIS) report on Bristol City's second division match with Millwall at Ashton Gate on 17 March 2001. "At 6.45pm the Millwall supporters were taken under escort towards the stadium," it reads. "As they passed a public house, a group of 30–40 males came out and bottles and glasses were thrown and pub windows smashed. After a short while it became apparent that both groups were from Millwall and each thought the other were City supporters."

Players themselves ought not be immune from this question, mind, especially when these anecdotes from Fulham's "player liaison officer" Mark Maunders in 2005 are taken into consideration. "Alain Goma once rang me sounding very troubled," he explained. "'Mark, Mark, I've got a big problem.' So I rushed straight over, and there he was, pointing at a fish bowl. 'You've got to help me,' he says, 'it's my goldfish – they're swimming in the wrong direction.'" As for Fabrice Fernandes, who complained of getting wet at night: "When I got to his bedroom, a window above his pillow was wide open. It's fair to say he wasn't the brightest spark."

"Has there ever been a case where a fan gave their jersey to a player before or during a game because the kit man forgot to pack a spare?"

The answer to this question of sartorial silliness is … yes. The first to take a step down the catwalk of shame was the former Bolton midfielder Djibril Diawara. After he was called up late to Sam Allardyce's squad to face Arsenal in September 2001, the knickers of kit man Russell Byrne-Fraser went all-a-twist as the kit had been sent south the day before without Diawara's jersey. Byrne-Fraser rustled up a replacement shirt by swapping a training top with Bolton fan Lee Houghton at Arsenal tube station. After name and number was ironed on at the Gunners' club shop, it all ended happily when Diawara came on as a substitute. "When I took the shirt off I was holding in my beer belly to see if they wanted me to go the whole hog and sit on the bench," said the 34-year-old postman. "I don't know what size Diawara is, but I'm 14st and my shirt looked tight on him." A grateful Allardyce added: "Djibril's a big lad so we needed to find somebody who had an extra large top. Fortunately, Lee fitted that bill." As a reward, Houghton was presented with his original shirt, complete with autographs from all the Bolton players, after the Trotters had bagged a 1-1 draw at Highbury.

Tracey Hunt, a baker from Salisbury, was another unlikely saviour, coming to the, ahem, knead of Bournemouth in 1999 when an SOS was sent out to a supporters' coach bound for Notts County. According to the Guardian, kit manager Bernie Morton had packed two shirts for striker Steve Fletcher but none for his namesake Carl. Hunt gladly handed over her top, to which the appropriate lettering was added, not that it helped much: the Cherries lost 5-1, with Carl Fletcher substituted at half-time.

"Cardiff City are famously the only non-English club to win the FA Cup, back in 1927. Are there any other 'foreign' clubs that have won domestic cup or league competitions?"

Even if the Bluebirds' FA Cup-winning feat is unequalled in this country (they almost repeated the feat in 2008, while Scottish side Queen's Park were runners-up in 1884 and 1885), they are not the only Welsh club to win silverware in English football. Step forward Swansea City (Division Three South champions in 1924-25 and 1948-49, third division champions in 1999-2000 and League One champions in 2007-08) and Wrexham (Division Three champions in 1977-78 and LDV Trophy winners in 2004-05). Conversely, before the League of Wales was created, English clubs routinely won the Welsh Cup. Oswestry United were the first in 1884, followed by Shrewsbury Town, Telford United (as Wellington), Chester City, Bristol City, Crewe Alexandra, Tranmere Rovers, South Liverpool and Hereford United. Another English club, Berwick Rangers, also deserves a mention, having won the 1978-79 Scottish second division title.

Northern Ireland side Derry City have played in the Republic's League of Ireland since 1985, winning the FAI Premier Division twice, in 1988-89 and 1996-97, the FAI Cup in 1988-89, 1994-95 and 2001-02 and 2005-06, plus the League of Ireland Cup on nine occasions, as well as one first division championship. Belfast outfit Alton United were also FAI Cup winners in 1923.

Moving further afield, there is the well-known principality in the south of France, where AS Monaco have won seven Ligue 1 titles, five Coupe de France trophies and one Coupe de la Ligue. They even pulled off the double in 1962-63. And there is also the impact of the Third Reich, which prompted Austrian pair Rapid Vienna (1938) and First Vienna (1943) to win the German Cup, as well as Rapid's 1941 German league triumph.

"On Wikipedia it states: 'The supporters of Rotherham United still maintain the record for the most pies consumed at a football match, with a consumption of pies 40% above the Football League average.' Is this true?"

Never one to shirk a challenge, the Knowledge got on the phone to find out if the Millers really can lay claim to being the pie capital of English football. And the answer is ... yes – well, sort of. Though Rotherham (average attendance at the time of writing in 2009-10: 3,480) clearly don't shift pastry in the same numbers as the Premier League giants, in terms of the pie-eating percentage of those coming through the gates at Don Valley they are top of the league.

"Among the 35-40 clubs we supply, you usually get 15-20% of supporters at the ground buying a pie," explained Peter Mayes of Pukka Pies. "At Rotherham that jumps to 40-50%. So, relatively, they're our best-performing football customer. They do like their pies."

But, of course, no pie-based coronation could be complete without reference to Wigan, whose Pooles Pies often come up trumps in fan surveys and, slightly weirdly, are now available in the region's health clubs. Pooles owner Dave Whelan (also the former Wigan chairman and the head of DW Sports Fitness) declared: "When you train you need to get energy back in your body, and if you're looking for something to eat, there's nothing better."

Tom Dickinson, in his book 92 Pies, also gave a thumps up to the pie credentials of Morecambe. But while Rotherham may not have the definitive crown, they certainly have a legitimate claim to the throne.

"What on earth was the Mercantile Credit Football Festival?"

Destined for a dusty shelf next to the Watney Cup, the Texaco Cup and the Anglo-Scottish Cup, the little-known Mercantile Credit Football Festival was part of the Football League's spectacular centenary celebrations in 1988. Played at Wembley over the weekend of 16-17 April, it involved 16 teams battling it out in a series of 40-minute knock-out matches (a move that ensured many games went to penalties – only eight goals were scored in the eight first-round games).

Nottingham Forest were the winners (and they proudly record that fact on their website). Having swatted aside Leeds 3-0 in the first round with goals from Franz

Carr, Stuart Pearce and Garry Parker, they beat Aston Villa on penalties in the quarter-finals after a 0-0 draw, surprise package Tranmere on penalties in the semis after a thrilling 2-2 draw with goals from Carr and Neil Webb, and Sheffield Wednesday – you've guessed it – on penalties with Webb scoring the decisive spot-kick after a goalless draw in the final – all this despite the absence of their manager, Brian Clough. In essence, the tournament proved to be something of an elongated shoot-out: nine of the 15 ties went to penalties and the crowd dwindled from a healthy 41,500 on the first day to a miserable 17,000 on day two, but it did provide Forest with a shiny new trinket for the cabinet and £75,000 for the coffers.

It provided the finale, if that is the right word, to almost a year of celebratory events, one of which was a match between a Football League XI and a Rest of the World XI in August 1987. A game that had the Guardian spluttering in a leader column that "soccer in August is not just an absurdity, it verges on the immoral". The 60,000 fans who turned out at Wembley to watch two star-studded line-ups probably disagreed.

Football League XI: Peter Shilton (Derby County), Richard Gough (Tottenham), Kenny Sansom (Arsenal), John McClelland (Watford), Paul McGrath (Manchester United), Liam Brady (West Ham), Bryan Robson (Manchester United), Neil Webb (Nottingham Forest), Clive Allen (Tottenham), Peter Beardsley (Liverpool), Chris Waddle (Tottenham). Substitutes: Steve Ogrizovic

(Coventry), Steve Clarke (Chelsea), Pat Nevin (Everton), Osvaldo Ardiles (QPR), Norman Whiteside (Manchester United), Alan Smith (Arsenal). Manager: Bobby Robson.

Rest of the World XI: Rinat Dasaev (USSR), Josimar (Brazil), Celso (Portugal), Julio Alberto (Spain), Glenn Hysen (Sweden), Salvatori Bagni (Italy), Thomas Berthold (West Germany), Gary Lineker (England), Michel Platini (France), Maradona (Argentina), Paulo Futre (Portugal). Substitutes: Andoni Zubizarreta (Spain), Lajos Detari (Hungary), Dragan Stojkovic (Yugoslavia), Igor Belanov (USSR), Preben Elkjær Larsen (Denmark), Lars Larsson (Sweden), Alexandre Zavarov (USSR). Manager: Terry Venables.

"I'm sure I heard a radio feature that claimed a Hearts squad in the 1990s boasted players called Holmes, Watson and Moriarty. Is this true?"

Alas, it seems you either misheard the report or you listen to a station staffed by unscrupulous mythmongers. While it is true that both Derek Holmes and Andy Watson have turned out for the Jambos during the 90s, they were not at the club at the same time. Neither the Knowledge nor the friendly folk we talked to at Tynecastle could find any record of the mysterious Moriarty having been on their books around that time.

As for other literary combos, the numbers 2, 3 and 4

in Mexico's 2002 World Cup squad were worn by Messrs Gabriel (de Anda), (Rafael) García and (Rafael) Márquez, respectively. But beyond that, the best we could come up with was Port Vale's strike force during the 1980s of Bob (Newton) and (John) Ridley, the brewers' that supply Coronation Street's Rovers Return Inn.

"What are the most unusual non-playing injuries suffered by footballers?"

The list, while not endless, is so long that Alan Hansen even released a book on the subject in 2009. Therefore, the following instances are merely the strangest of the strange, rather than a comprehensive collection:

Richard Wright: As good a player as any to begin with, simply because outrageous misfortune has visited him on two separate occasions. Back in the summer of 2003, while packing away his suitcases after a family holiday, the Everton goalkeeper tumbled out of his loft and damaged his right shoulder. "I'm not superstitious," said Wright, "but the accident was on Friday the 13th and I am going to be careful now what I do on certain dates." Perhaps this extra caution took his eye off the ball and led to the second incident, at Chelsea on 8 February 2006. While warming up for the Toffees' FA Cup replay, Wright failed to heed a wooden goalmouth warning sign that requested he prepare elsewhere. The former England keeper moved said sign into the net and, as the Guardian's account of the match details, "fell on it when he stretched to make a save, turning his ankle".

Alan Wright: The Aston Villa left-back, all 5ft 4in of him, strained his knee ligaments while stretching to reach the pedals in his new Ferrari. "The accelerator's position meant my right leg was bent slightly and my knee was giving me grief," recalled Wright, who sensibly downgraded to a Rover 416 soon after.

Kirk Broadfoot: Poaching an egg ought not be such a dangerous pastime, but the Rangers and Scotland defender suffered facial burns after two of them exploded in his face after he had cooked them in a microwave. "The accident was no joke, I could have lost my eyesight," declared Broadfoot in the wake of inevitable "egg on his face" headlines in 2009. "There was boiling water and glass in my face."

Svein Grøndalen: While diligently out on a training run in a Norwegian forest during the 1970s, international defender Grøndalen encountered a dozing moose, which did not take too kindly to being stirred from its slumber. After the moose charged at him, Grøndalen took cover by diving down a hill, whereby he suffered a nasty gash in his left leg that would subsequently rule him out of Norway's international against Finland.

Darius Vassell: If you ever needed a reason not to practise DIY surgery, this is it. Attempting to burst a blood blister underneath the nail of a big toe in November 2002, Vassell opted to use … a drill. "I am not certain he looks after his feet properly," deadpanned his Aston Villa manager Graham Taylor after Vassell got an infection in the wound and lost his toenail.

Rowan Fernández: The then-Kaizer Chiefs goalkeeper, nicknamed "Spider" owing to his fascination with creepy crawlies, got a little too up close and personal with one of them in 2003. "I had just finished cleaning the house and a small spider bit me on my foot," he recalled. "I spent a week in hospital and lost 14kg."

Norbert Nigbur: The Schalke and Germany goalkeeper's trip to a restaurant in 1980 set in motion a chain of events that would ultimately end with the near-destruction of poor Patrick Battiston. Out for dinner with his fiancée, Nigbur managed to tear his knee cartilage while attempting to get up from his table, ruling himself out of the European Championships. Into his shoes stepped Harald Schumacher and two years later, well, you know the rest.

Milan Rapaic: The Croatia international missed the start of Hajduk Split's 1995-96 season after poking himself in the eye with a boarding pass at an airport.

John Durnin: Playing a round of golf with Portsmouth team-mate Alan McLoughlin, Durnin overturned the pair's buggy while cruising down the fairway and dislocated his elbow, ruling him out of action for six weeks. "People think we must have been larking about, but me and Macca like our golf and we weren't being silly or anything like that," explained Durnin.

Christian Okpala: "He permanently provoked me by farting all the time." So went the defence of Okpala's Stuttgart Kickers team-mate Sascha Bender, who punched him in the face.

Lionel Letizi: The PSG goalkeeper injured muscles in his back while playing one particularly physical game of … Scrabble. "I completely put my back out," admitted a sheepish Letizi, who had been attempting to pick up a letter tile that had fallen to the floor back in December 2002.

Kevin Kyle: The Scotland striker was whisked off to hospital in March 2006 after a feeding session with his eight-month-old son Max ended with the youngster knocking a jug of boiling water on to his father's lap, scalding the Sunderland man's testicles. A similar fate once befell Rochdale's Kieran Durkan when team-mate Richard Green managed to spill a boiling kettle on his lap, while the Preston midfielder Dean Barrick once had a waitress spill hot coffee on a similarly sensitive area of his.

Mistar: Tragically, the Indonesian player was trampled to death by a herd of feral pigs that invaded his club's practice pitch during a training session.

"Wikipedia claims that a former Lazio midfielder called Luciano Re Cecconi apparently met his demise while 'pretending to rob a friend's jewellery shop as a practical joke'. Did this really happen?"

"*L'Angelo Biondo*" (The Blond Angel) was an integral part of Lazio's first-ever Serie A title-winning side from 1974, but the dashing box-to-box midfielder would tragically meet his maker just four years later, in the most farcical of circumstances. Walking into a Rome jewellery shop with team-mate Piero Ghedin, Re Cecconi decided to play a prank. "Stop!" he screamed, with his hands in his pockets. "This is a robbery!" The jeweller, Bruno Tabocchini, who had his back turned, spun round and pointed a pistol at Ghedin, who swiftly put his hands up. Re Cecconi did not and was shot. "It's a joke, it's a joke," gasped Re Cecconi. Within 30 minutes, he was dead.

"I'm interested in English football between the wars and was wondering if you could tell me how the teams travelled in those times. Was it all by train or also by bus? And did the stars like Hughie Gallacher and Dixie Dean make enough money to buy their own cars?"

As far as we can ascertain, players like Dean and Gallacher travelled to and from matches on public transport. Certainly, in the days before the maximum wage, they were not afforded the sort of sums that allowed them to purchase top-of-the-range vehicles, so unless players came from a seriously well-to-do background, it was the bus or the train for them. Indeed, Dean's eventual replacement at Goodison Park, the England international Tommy Lawton, often told stories of how Evertonians (and his tram conductor) would wish him well on the way to matches – while telling him he would "never be as good as Dean". ("Well, that's charming," was Lawton's response.)

Coincidentally, motor vehicles and trains played a massive part in the lives of the two players in question. Dean fractured his skull, cheekbone and jaw coming off a motorbike in June 1926 ("I went right through the windscreen of the car"), injuries that were thought by doctors to have ended the 19-year-old's life, let alone his career, almost before it had begun. He was unconscious for 36 hours and had to have a metal plate inserted in his head but, soon enough, he was up and about, scoring 60 goals in the 1927-28 season.

Gallacher's case was altogether more tragic. The Scotland forward, whose goals led Newcastle to the league title in 1926-27, was sold to Chelsea against his will in 1930, and some say he was never the same again. He eventually returned to Tyneside to play for Gateshead, but drink and personal problems took a hold. In May 1957, seven years after the death of his beloved second wife Hannah, Gallacher was accused of mistreating his son Matthew (sports historian Paul Joannou told the Independent in 1999 that "people who knew him were convinced that it was all nonsense. They knew that he would never harm his lads. But the shame contained in the very accusation of child abuse and neglect was too much for him"). Depressed and despondent, Gallacher visited the train tracks near his house, at a spot known in the area as Dead Man's Crossing, and walked in front of the York to Edinburgh train. He was 54.

"While listening to Eddy Grant's 1982 album Killer on the Rampage, I noticed that the singer had name checked Diego Maradona on the sleeve notes. Can anyone shed any light on the Grant-Maradona lost years?"

We are not exactly sure how the unlikely friendship arose, but as early as 1979, at Grant's "Live at Luna Park, Buenos Aires" pre-Falklands War concert, a young Maradona joined the dreadlock star on stage. Video footage of the appearance can be found on the bonus DVD from the 2008 "deluxe edition" reissue of Grant's Walking on Sunshine album. As for the later Killer on the Rampage acknowledgement, Grant writes: "Special thanks to Diego Armando Maradonna (sic) and his family for their special friendship."

"After watching Matt Holland and Stephen Ireland in action, I was wondering if a team could be comprised entirely of national teams?"

Wonder no more, for we have assembled a vast horde of players that could get into such a team. Purely subjectively, here is our favourite starting XI, lining up in a 4-4-2 formation, followed by a list of other potentials. As you will see, we have been particularly pedantic regarding the omissions of Pat, Phil and Matt "Holland", Stephen "Ireland" and José Luis González "China". Sadly, we were unable to find any players with the surnames "Netherlands", "Republic of Ireland" or "People's Republic of China" – which, according to Fifa, are the team's official names.

Manager: Rinus Israël (DWS, Feyenoord, Excelsior, Zwolle, Netherlands, and formerly in charge of the Ghana national side).

Assistant: Joe Jordan (Greenock Morton, Leeds United, Manchester United, Milan, Verona, Southampton, Bristol

City, Scotland, the manager of Bristol City, Hearts and Stoke City, and the assistant manager at Portsmouth and Tottenham).

Goalkeeper: George Poland (Cardiff City, Wrexham).

Defenders: Alan Oman (Northampton Town); Gino Brazil (Shamrock Rovers, Bohemians); Mike England (Blackburn, Tottenham, Cardiff City, Seattle Sounders, Wales – player and manager); Jack France (Stalybridge Celtic, Bath City, Swindon Town, Halifax Town).

Midfielders: Danilo Portugal (Goiás, Vitória Setubal, Ponte Preta); Gaël Germany (Samaritaine, Martinique); Ryan France (Alfreton Town, Hull City, Sheffield United); Mirko Benin (Varese, Fiorentina, Como, Cremonese).

Strikers: Jason Scotland (San Juan Jabloteh, Defence Force, St Johnstone, Dundee United, Swansea City, Wigan Athletic, Trinidad & Tobago); Zay Angola (Academica Coimbra, Stoke City).

Best of the rest – goalkeepers: Michael Jordan (Arsenal, Chesterfield, Lewes, Stevenage Borough, Eastbourne Borough, Farnborough), Matt Jordan (Dallas Burn, Odense, Colombus Crew, Montreal Impact). Defenders: Ken Oman (Bohemians, Derry City); Chris Scotland (Stirling Albion); Andy Jordan (Bristol City, Cardiff City, Hartlepool United); Tom Jordan (Southend United,

Tamworth, Forest Green Rovers). Midfielders: Stephen Jordan (Manchester City, Burnley); Lee Poland (Northwich Victoria, Altrincham); Tal Benin (Maccabi Haifa, Hapoel Haifa, Brescia, Maccabi Tel Aviv, Israel); Scott Jordan (York City, Scarborough). Strikers: Alan Brazil (Ipswich Town, Tottenham, Manchester United, Coventry City, QPR, Scotland); Alan Brazil (Arbroath, Stenhousemuir); Somalia (Feyenoord); Israel (Real Betis); Biko Brazil (FC Den Bosch, RKC Waalwijk, FC Omniworld, Apep Pitsilia, Dessel Sport); Edwin Congo (Once Caldas, Real Madrid, Levante, Sporting Gijón, Recreativo Huelva, Olympic Xàtiva, Colombia); Gary Wales (Hamilton Academical, Hearts, Gillingham, Kilmarnock, Raith Rovers).

"Charlie Mitten once scored three penalties in a game for Manchester United against Aston Villa in 1950. Has anyone else ever managed this unusual hat-trick?"

Ronaldo is probably the highest-profile player to have matched Mitten's achievement, after scoring all the goals during a 3-1 World Cup qualifier against Argentina in June 2004. Not only did the big-boned forward win all three spot-kicks (fouled by Gabriel Heinze, Javier Mascherano and then goalkeeper Pablo Cavallero), he got straight back up to beat Cavallero on each occasion. "Actually, it was four penalties," noted Ronaldo after his first successful effort was disallowed for a team-mate's encroachment.

Next up is Andy Blair, who scored three from the spot for Sheffield Wednesday in their 4-2 Milk Cup win against Luton in November 1984, the first time the feat had been achieved in the League Cup. Jan Molby followed this up against Coventry in November 1986, before David Dunn did likewise for Blackburn Rovers against Rochdale in September 2000. The 2004 FA Vase quarter-final between Bideford AFC and Gosport County also witnessed the Devon side's Mike Southgate grab a penalty treble.

As for the Football League, Ken Barnes registered the top-flight's first ever penalty hat-trick in the December 1957 6-2 thrashing of Everton, while Hibernian's Eddie Turnbull bagged three of his four goals against Celtic in February 1950 from the spot. Paraguayan extrovert José Luis Chilavert became the first goalkeeper to score three penalties, during Vélez Sársfield's 6-1 Argentinian league victory over Ferro Carril Oeste in November 1999. But it is the Cruzeiro striker Alex who can lay claim to an even more spectacular record: during the final game of the 2003 Brazilian Championship, Cruzeiro put the seal on their title triumph with a 7-0 spanking of Bahia, the first four goals of which came in the opening 38 minutes from the spot, each from Alex's boot.

Before we leave the subject, though, special mention must go to the Argentina striker Martin Palermo, whose name can be found in the Guinness Book of Records for missing the most penalties in a single game. In July 1999, during the 3-0 Copa América defeat to Colombia, Palermo conspired to miss three times from the spot. No wonder

Colombia's coach Javier Alvarez couldn't believe his luck. "There's always a first time for everything – and today I saw it," he said afterwards, stifling a chuckle.

"I heard that Juventus took their colours from Notts County. Is this true and, if so, are there any other clubs' kits that have been inspired by different teams?"

We might as well begin with Arsenal, who pinched their dark red shirts from Nottingham Forest. According to Arsenal's official website, "a small group of Nottingham Forest players, Fred Beardsley, Bill Parr and Charlie Bates joined Dial Square FC (the club's first name) and brought their old red kit along with them. Working to a tight budget, the club decided the most inexpensive way of acquiring a strip was to kit out the team in the same colour as the ex-Forest players."

In turn, Sparta Prague (or Athletic Club Sparta, as they were initially known) based their dark red top on the Gunners' shirt (after their president Dr Otakar Petrić visited London in 1906), while Ajax's 1911 kit owed its white shorts to Arsenal's early look. When he arrived in 1925, manager Herbert Chapman came up with their more familiar look after spotting someone at the ground wearing a red sleeveless sweater over a white shirt. And that itself has since been copied by Portuguese club Sporting Braga, themselves even nicknamed the Arsenalists. North London rivals Tottenham have not always come up with their own original kits either, mind, with what are believed to be tributes to Blackburn Rovers' blue and white halved jerseys and Preston's white shirts and navy blue shorts around the turn of the 19th century.

At around the same time, Crystal Palace were borrowing their claret and blue strip from Aston Villa – literally; the Villans lent them some kit (and a secretary) when they first got up and running in the early 1900s. In the 1970s, manager Malcolm Allison changed Palace's shirt to the red and blue stripes we know (and changed their nickname from "Glaziers" to "Eagles"). Allison had already been responsible for Manchester City's red and black shirts in 1969, deciding during his stint as assistant manager that it would turn them into Milan. It worked – for a while – with City lifting the FA Cup, League Cup and Cup Winners' Cup in the two seasons that they wore it.

Blackpool's famous tangerine top derives from Holland's colours, after club director and international referee Albert Hargreaves officiated an international between the Dutch and Belgium in the mid-1920s and suggested the club follow suit. Roy Calley's Blackpool: A Complete Record 1887-1992 notes that while the orange shirt was well received by fans, the black elements of the kit (shorts, collar, cuffs) were ditched in 1925 after players complained about not standing out clearly enough.

North of the border, Celtic's famous shirts are understood to have been inspired by Scotland's first Irish club, Hibernian (from *Hibernia*, the Latin name for Ireland), who wore the green and white hoops (and the Irish harp) from their inception in 1875. But Queen's Park surely enjoy the bragging rights, having had their colours adopted by Scotland. "Queen's Park instigated the first ever known international fixture when they played England in Glasgow on St Andrew's Day in 1872," states the club website. "The Scotland team comprised entirely of Queen's Park players, who wore their club jerseys – dark blue in colour, the same colours as worn today by the national team." Subsequently, Millwall Rovers took inspiration from Scotland's dark blue kit when a mixture of Scottish and English workers from Morton's Jam Factory on the Isle of Dogs founded the club in 1885. According to James Murray's book Lions of the South, they "were convinced they could form a football team to give other local clubs a tough time". Indeed.

Moving to the continent, the history of Barcelona's famous shirt is far from black and white. Legend has it that the famous flagrant blue and red shirts come from FC Basel's colours, since their founder – Hans Gamper (later to adopt the Catalan name, Joan) – was Swiss and had played for them. "Sadly there is no historical document proving that Barcelona's shirts were based on Basel's, but the circumstantial evidence is quite compelling," said Hans-Dieter Gerber, the leader of the Swiss Sport Museum, in 2008. "The fact that Gamper went to Spain and set up FC Barcelona who started playing with the same distinctive colours he had played in while captaining Basel suggests the story is at least credible."

However, in his history of the club, Barça, writer Jimmy Burns contends that it was in fact one of the club's first players, Englishman Arthur Witty, who exported the colours from Merseyside – Crosby's Merchant Taylor's School, to be precise. "Arthur claimed he drew on his old school colours for the maroon and blue that were to become Barça's," writes Burns. "In correspondence with Arthur's son Frederick in 1975, the school's then-headmaster Reverend HM Luft reinforced this claim. In a letter, which I have seen, Reverend Luft states: 'I think it is very likely that the present colours of FC Barcelona are ultimately derived from our original colours here.'"

And if you thought there was something of Sweden in Boca Juniors' yellow and blue colours, you would be right. After losing a play-off against local rivals Boedo for the right to their black-and-white-striped kit in March 1907, Boca agreed to visit Buenos Aires harbour and take the colours of the first foreign ship to come in. The 4,146-tonne freighter Drottning Sophia arrived from Copenhagen, flying the Swedish flag and the rest is history. When the club released a limited-edition 105th anniversary shirt earlier in 2010, it even bore the yellow and blue national flag on the front.

But what about Juventus, as the question states? Well, back in 1903, Juve were sick of their fancy pink shirts fading in the wash, so asked an English player at the club, John Savage, for help. One call from Savage to a Notts County-supporting friend later and the Old Lady had the kit she still sports to this very day.

"Have any players ever been punished for being sarcastic?"

There are a fair few, arguably the most famous of which being one Paul Gascoigne. While playing for Rangers in the 7-0 rout of Hibernian in December 1995, Gazza was jogging back towards the halfway line at a goal-kick. Spotting that rookie referee Dougie Smith had dropped his yellow card, Gascoigne picked it up, before cheekily waving it at the official – who waved it right back in his face. The booking took the jovial Geordie over the maximum disciplinary points, earning him a two-match ban. "He actually looked for his [card] to book me because he thought I'd brought my own on the park with me," Gascoigne would later recall in the Sunday Mail. "It didn't sicken me off because I just felt embarrassed for him."

Another to fall foul of a thoroughly humourless official was the Crystal Palace midfielder Joonas Kolkka. During his team's 3-2 defeat at Liverpool in November 2004, the Finn grew tired of what he perceived to be Milan Baros's propensity for going down with a bout of play-acting. After one such incident, Kolkka attempted to make his point by theatrically throwing himself to the floor in front of referee Phil Dowd. End result: Kolkka booked and Baros scoring the second of his eventual hat-trick from the resultant free-kick.

If Kolkka's caper was at least inventive, Wayne Rooney's sardonic applause of referee Kim Milton Nielsen awarding him a booking against Villarreal in September 2005 (securing him an immediate second yellow and an early bath – "even sarcastic play is not allowed," said Nielsen) has proved imitable. A display of insincere applause from Real Betis's Ricardo Oliveira during their game against Barcelona in the same month swiftly resulted in him receiving his marching orders.

The seemingly-soon-to-be-former Manchester City forward Robinho was once booked during his original Santos days for humiliating defenders with too many step-overs, while his team-mate at City, Carlos Tevez, was sent off for performing the "chicken dance" after scoring for Boca Juniors in the Copa Libertadores semi-final second leg against River Plate in 2004. On paper it may not seem like the greatest of sins, but for the fact that Boca fans repeatedly taunt their River rivals as "gallinas" (hens) since the 1960s when they "chickened out" of a series of title wins when well placed. Tevez walked, but still managed to make the referee hilariously repeat the gesture three times by way of explanation. Boca later won on penalties.

"Which is the smallest football league in the world, how many teams does it have and how many times do they meet each season?"

We must look 28 miles beyond the south-western tip of Great Britain for this answer, where the Isles of Scilly Football League takes place each year – consisting of just two teams. Woolpack Wanderers – the 2009 champions – and Garrison Gunners meet on 16 occasions in the league each season, as well as separate matches in the annual Old Man's Game, Wholesalers Cup and the two-legged Foredeck Cup. The Wanderers and the Gunners took their names in 1984, from the two surviving teams that had played on the islands since the 1950s (the Rangers and the Rovers), but football on the Scillies can be traced as far back as the post-WW1 Lyonesse Inter-Island Cup, when St Mary's, Tresco, St Martins, Bryher and St Agnes all competed.

"People think we're crazy but the league works," said boat builder and Wanderers striker Andy Hicks (formerly of the Gunners) in a 2007 Telegraph feature. "Every Sunday's a fresh challenge. You'd be amazed how close it is. Five times in the last eight years the championship's been decided on the final day."

"What is the weirdest kick-off ever taken?"

One of the more memorable would have to be Scotland's away World Cup qualifier against Estonia in October 1996. On the morning of the game, Fifa ordered the match to be brought forward by three hours because of inadequate floodlights; citing insufficient notice, the home side refused to turn up, leaving Scotland with no opposition. And they still didn't win. The game kicked off on the stroke of 3pm when Billy Dodds passed to John

Collins, three seconds before referee Miroslav Radoman blew to end the farce, as the travelling Scottish fans chanted: "One team in Tallinn, there's only one team in Tallinn." Despite Estonia's behaviour, Fifa instructed that the match be replayed at a neutral venue, when the Scots were held 0-0 in Monaco.

Then there was the August 2004 Carling Cup first-round tie between Yeovil and Plymouth. After defender Graham Coughlan sustained an injury, Lee Johnson's attempt to return the ball to the Pilgrims' goalkeeper Luke McCormick failed spectacularly, the ball accidentally sailing into the net. The Yeovil manager Gary Johnson responded by allowing Argyle's striker Stevie Crawford to take the ensuing kick-off unchallenged and run all the way from the centre circle and put the ball into an empty net. "I made an on-the-spot decision and I'm pleased I made the right decision," said Johnson Sr, whose honourable gesture must have been good karma: his son Lee went on to complete a hat-trick and secure his side a 3-2 victory.

Even more comical was the goal that Hans-Jorg Butt conceded for Bayer Leverkusen during his team's 3-2 win at Schalke in April 2004. Celebrating the third goal just that little too much, the penalty-taking goalkeeper failed to notice the referee return the ball to Schalke; Ebbe Sand played the ball to Mike Hanke, who fired into the unguarded net from the halfway line. "I didn't think the referee would allow them to kick off so quickly," admitted a red-faced Butt afterwards.

"Can anyone clarify what is actually shouted on the classic opening credits of Football Italia as it was on Channel 4, 'gol, lazoo ...' or something. And what does it mean in English?"

The British Council's website, strangely, divulged the real answer. "When Channel 4 televised live Italian football in the 1990s, the opening credits had a typical piece of Italian commentary exclaiming *'Golaccio!!!'*" it notes. "Interestingly, although this phrase sounds Italian, it isn't. It actually comes from a kind of folk memory of what Latin commentators sound like. Programme makers Chrysalis reveal that the man who wrote the theme music, Steve Duberry [along with Ben Chapman], 'sort of imagined it from a phantom Brazilian/Italian memory' and recorded it as part of the music. If you had to translate it, it would be something like 'goaltastic'." Incidentally, the theme's music was taken from the 7" edit version of I'm Stronger Now, written by Chapman and Duberry, performed by the Definitive Two and released in 1992 on the Deconstruction label.

"Where does the word 'nutmeg' come from?"

There are several possible answers, beginning with the thought that nutmeg is 1940s Cockney rhyming slang for leg. However, in his superb book Football Talk: The Language and Folklore of the World's Greatest Game,

Peter Seddon offers a far more likely etymology: that it derives from duplicitous procedure in the nutmeg trade. As he points out, the verb "nutmegged" is listed by the Oxford English Dictionary as "arising in the 1870s which in Victorian slang came to mean 'to be tricked or deceived, especially in a manner which makes the victim look foolish'."

The word arose because of a sharp practice used in nutmeg exports between America and England. "Nutmegs were such a valuable commodity that unscrupulous exporters were wont to pull a fast one by mixing a helping of wooden replicas into the sacks being shipped to England," writes Seddon. "Being nutmegged soon came to imply stupidity on the part of the duped victim and cleverness on the part of the trickster."

Considering that so much of football's language dates from its formative years, that seems the most likely explanation. It certainly sounds more convincing than Jimmy Hill's claim that the word was coined during the 1940s to describe the skill of placing the ball between an opponent's legs before retrieving it on the other side. Or indeed the suggestion made in Alex Leith's book, Over the Moon, Brian: The Language of Football, that nuts – a term commonly used for nutmeg in the north of England – "refers to the testicles of the player through whose legs the ball has been passed, and nutmeg is just a development from this".

"Do many footballers actually complete their military service, in countries that have conscription, of course?"

While the lack of conscription in Britain these days has saved the likes of Joey Barton from some timely national service, many of the biggest names on the continent have not been as lucky. Take those in Serie A, for instance, as the ever-helpful James Richardson kindly explained. "Italian stars of a suitable age were indeed part of the leva, or conscription," he said. "I myself recall visiting the special Napoli barracks set up to house them and other athletes, and meeting Fabio Galante, Alessandro Del Piero, Fabio Cannavaro and Marco Delvecchio. I say 'house' but they actually spent comparatively little time there, club commitments calling them away for the majority of the week. Conscription has now been phased out in Italy, but back in those days the Italian army even had its own football team, who never really won anything – in keeping with local military traditions, one might say. They did stop short of changing sides at half-time, mind."

South Korean footballers, like all men in the country, are also subject to 26 months of military service before the age of 30. However, after their run to the World Cup semi-finals in 2002, the squad saw their conscription time slashed to just one month. "The Defence Ministry plans to positively consider and actively promote ways of giving the players favours in the form of exempting them from military duty," said a national ministry spokesman. Ten players benefited from relaxing of the law, though they could have dodged the draft completely with the help of a tattoo parlour; South Korea's law rules that men with body art are unfit for the military as they cause "abomination among fellow soldiers".

There have also been several high-profile national service escapees. Roma left-back John Arne Riise was due to join the Norwegian army, before his agent Einar Baardsen clarified the situation. "As long as you are working or playing football abroad you are automatically excluded from any military service," Baardsen told the BBC in 2002. "I'm sure the military service would love to have him but it will take many years before they can draft him. And if he stays outside the country until he is 28 he will never be drafted." Hence, Riise will never now be signed up. Unless he wants to, of course. Shefki Kuqi also steered clear of a six-month tour of duty back in Finland, again by means of leaving his homeland. "Fortunately my lawyer sorted it all out and I didn't have to go back," he said back in the summer of 2005. "I got away with it because I've been living abroad."

"My brother and I have spent many hours arguing over Lee Dixon. I swear blind that the man has scored more than 60 career goals, but he maintains that Dixon couldn't finish a hot dinner. Who is right?"

All those hours spent arguing over Lee Dixon – surely you had better things to do, like the ironing? – were a waste of time, because you are both wide of the mark. During his 20-year career, Dixon played 815 matches for Burnley, Chester City, Bury, Stoke City and Arsenal, scoring 39 times – a figure that sadly does not include a legendary 40-yard pearler of an own goal against Coventry in September 1991.

"[He] went with an American company once called Brooks," then-team-mate Perry Groves explained to footy-boots.com. "They were trying to get into the UK football boot market, but theirs were worse than Woolworths' football boots. Dixon was wearing them in training and we were all taking the micky. Normally he'd ditch them, but because he was being paid to wear them, he didn't want to. Anyway, Dicko was wearing these boots for the first time against Coventry, had the ball in the right-back position, without any pressure. He went to flight the ball back to Seaman, but instead managed to lob the ball over him for an own goal. He never wore the football boots again."

Nonetheless, by our calculations that still rates as a goal almost every 21 games. OK, so he was not quite Thierry Henry, but for a defender, his record is not too bad.

By contrast, Nigel Winterburn – Dixon's long-time full-back partner at Highbury – scored just 21 goals in his 857 professional matches.

"The whole Wayne Bridge–John Terry saga set me thinking about players who were team-mates despite being sworn enemies. Are there any others?"

In-fighting? Team-mates at war? Holland seems like the obvious place to begin. Trouble in the Dutch camp goes way back, with tension between Ajax players and non-Ajax players alleged as far back as at the 1974 World Cup due to money raised from advertising not being pooled equally among the squad. Two years later, on the eve of the Euro 76 semi-final against Czechoslovakia, PSV Eindhoven pair Jan van Beveren and Willy van der Kuylen walked out on the squad, citing the increased influence and power of Ajax's Johan Cruyff as the reason.

Perhaps the starkest example of Holland colleagues failing to get along, though, came at Euro 96. The problems at the tournament had been a long time brewing and the catalyst was the situation at Ajax, where young black players – Edgar Davids, Michael Reiziger and Patrick Kluivert among them – were being paid around 20% that of Ronald de Boer, Danny Blind and co. Clarence Seedorf, firm friends with Davids and Kluivert, had jumped ship to Sampdoria two years earlier after De Boer was handed the right-midfield role at Ajax when it had supposedly been promised to him. The latter blamed Blind, De Boer and the club's coach, Louis van Gaal.

With that background, it was little surprise that trouble flared in England. In his book Brilliant Orange: The Neurotic Genius of Dutch Football, David Winner notes that "the black players complained, with some justification, that [coach Guus] Hiddink did not listen to them, that they were not served Surinamese food in camp, and that Ajax paid them less than white players." Once the action began, though, things got no better. Blind, the captain, was suspended from the opening game against Scotland, but publicly criticised Seedorf and Davids after the disappointing goalless draw. Seedorf responded by criticising Blind's "lack of respect". When Davids was dropped for the subsequent game against Switzerland, he reacted by telling Dutch newspapers that Hiddink, "should not put his head in the ass of some players" – a reference to Davids's Ajax team-mates De Boer and Blind – and was summarily kicked out of the squad. But despite the exit of his friend and the ongoing animosity in the squad, Seedorf still managed an hour on the same pitch as Blind and De Boer in the quarter-final defeat to France, which Holland lost in a penalty shoot-out. The only player to miss his spot-kick? Seedorf.

Though the tension between Lothar Matthäus and Stefan Effenberg never manifested itself on the pitch either with Bayern Munich or the national side, the German midfielders never saw eye-to-eye. Effenberg reserved special opprobrium for Matthäus in his 2003 autobiography, I Showed Them All, calling his former national captain "a cheeky big mouth" and "a quitter", and including a chapter entitled "What Lothar Matthäus knows about football", which consisted simply of a blank page (perhaps an homage to The Clown Prince of Soccer, the 1955 memoirs of the Sunderland and England striker Len Shackleton, which contained a chapter headed "The average director's knowledge of football", followed by a similarly barren page). Effenberg's book also describes his relationship with wife Claudia, who he got together with when she was still married to his former team-mate Thomas Strunz. "You, pig, stole my wife!" fumed Strunz after discovering a text to Claudia from Effenberg.

As for on-field bust-ups, one of the more famous involved Charlton's Mike Flanagan and Derek Hales in an FA Cup third-round tie against Maidstone United, then of the Southern League, in January 1979. With five minutes remaining the scores were level: Hales made a run towards goal, Flanagan – the ball at his feet – delayed his pass and by the time Hales eventually received the ball, he had been caught offside. "Words were exchanged … and the two moved towards each other," wrote Keith Peacock, a team-mate of the pair, in his autobiography No Substitute. "They went head to head and Hales threw the first punch. He wasn't the kind of guy to see what the other fellow would do. Blows were exchanged." Both players were sent off (Charlton held on to draw 1-1 and secure a replay, which they won 2-1), but the incident had merely brought to a head something that had been bubbling below the surface.

"It was a bit more than that," said Hales, without elaborating, in 2005. "The manager should have sorted it out beforehand." Hales was sacked and then reinstated; Flanagan was fined and then submitted a transfer request, which pre-empted his £650,000 transfer to Crystal Palace. "I was seen as the nasty one," added Hales. "But it takes two to tango." The pair were reunited five years later when Flanagan rejoined the Addicks.

Finally, the West Brom cult hero Bob Taylor appeared to inadvertently be behind the breakdown of Andy Cole and Teddy Sheringham's relationship at Manchester United. The on-loan striker opened the scoring for Bolton Wanderers at Old Trafford back in February 1998, a goal that resulted in a dressing-room squabble between the United pair as to who was responsible. Cole refused to speak to his strike partner thereafter. However, according to an interview with Cole in Andy Mitten's book, Glory Glory, the contempt can be tracked even further back. "Our problems started when I made my England debut [against Uruguay in March 1995]," explained Cole. "I replaced Teddy. I was making my debut. Maybe I was naïve, but I think he should have wished me all the best. Instead he walked straight past me and blanked me. So I was devastated when Teddy Sheringham signed for United because I couldn't stand him."

As an interesting postscript, though, the Daily Mail reported in December 2009 that Cole, part of the England 2018 World Cup delegation on a trip to Nigeria, was asked to provide his own commentary on the last two minutes of the 1999 Champions League final video. "Cole singled out Sheringham for praise," claimed the account, "saying his reading of the game was very special, particularly his intuitive movement in the penalty area that could not be coached."

"Barcelona had not fallen behind in a game during the 2009-10 season prior to their defeat against Atlético Madrid. Is this a record? Unbeaten runs are one thing, but 21 games without ever having been a goal down?"

Remarkably, the statistical archives highlight two instances when Barça's achievement has been topped. In 2007-08, CSKA Sofia went 27 league games without falling behind, after doing so in the first game of the season. It was not until Enyo Krastovchev scored for Levski Sofia in the 29th game of the season that they were behind. Beating that, however, and overlapping two seasons from 9 November 2004 until 28 February 2006, Al-Ahly of Egypt went 32 league matches without going a goal down, before Ahmed Mohammadi scored for Ghazi Al Mehalla.

"I am having great difficulty in discovering the exact details of the speech that the Norwegian commentator made after Norway's unexpected victory against England in September 1981. I know that it includes the regurgitation of several important historical figures and ends with 'your boys took one hell of a beating'. What exactly did he say?"

The late Bjørge Lillelien was the man behind the microphone for Norwegian radio in Oslo that night as Norway recorded a 2-1 win, when he launched into the infamous following commentary, here translated in full:

"He blows the whistle! He blows the whistle! Norway has beaten England 2-1 in football! We are best in the world! We are best in the world! We've beaten England 2-1 in football. It's absolutely incredible! We have beaten England! England, birthplace of giants ... Lord Nelson, Lord Beaverbrook, Sir Winston Churchill, Sir Anthony Eden, Clement Attlee, Henry Cooper, Lady Diana ... we have beaten them all. We have beaten them all. Maggie Thatcher, can you hear me? Maggie Thatcher, I have a message for you: we have knocked England out of the football World Cup. Maggie Thatcher, as they say in your language in the boxing bars around Madison Square Garden in New York: your boys took a hell of a beating! Your boys took a hell of a beating!"

"Have any footballers revealed their transfer plans via a social networking website?"

Ashley-Paul Robinson's is arguably the most renowned example of a player publicising a move on t'internet before notifying his club. The 18-year-old winger revealed his plans to leave Crystal Palace for Fulham in July 2008 by posting a Facebook status update which his 194 friends could see. Unfortunately, so too could all 2.7m members of the site who had joined its London section, just like Robinson, who had unwittingly broken the story to supporters of both clubs and to anyone else in the capital interested in perusing candid transfer gossip. "Ashley-Paul is goin fulham on monday. If i pull dis off im on dis ting," read his rather eloquent message. A day later, he added: "Ashley-Paul is travling 2 Bath With Fulham Fingers Crossed." As news of the move spread, Robinson posted a new message: "Ashley-Paul has been very naughty lol!"

Palace, however, did not find Robinson's frankness a laughing matter. "It's pretty embarrassing for the club that this guy is telling the world he's looking to leave," a Palace source told the Guardian. "Perhaps someone should tell him to be a bit more private about what he's putting on the internet." A parting of the ways was inevitable. "We feel it's probably better that he looks elsewhere to further his career," clarified the Palace manager Neil Warnock. Fulham chose not to give Robinson a deal, while further fruitless trials at Hereford and Carlisle followed, before he signed for Conference South outfit Bromley in October 2008.

Robinson, however, is not the only footballer to experience the perils of the information super-highway. Leon Osborne, a 17-year-old trainee with Bradford City who had played just 10 minutes of first-team football, announced on his Bebo page in June 2007 that he was not particularly enamoured with the city, did not like the team, missed his home town of Doncaster (36 miles away) and was hoping for a move to a bigger club. Manager Stuart McCall met with Osborne and disciplined the youngster ("In future he will prove himself on the football field not on websites," sniffed McCall), while also forcing him to apologise in public to the club's fans. "I am truly sorry for what was said but it was never meant in that way," said a suitably chastened Osborne. "It was simply me trying to wind up my friends back home in Doncaster and it has backfired on me."

"Is it true that Harry Kewell could have played for England?"

Thanks to his father Rod being born in England, the fact that Kewell himself was born in Sydney's western suburbs, where he also grew up, would not have hampered his eligibility and he could have worn the three lions. Playing for the Socceroos against Iran in a World Cup qualifying play-off at the age of 17, however, did.

Having been invited to train with Leeds as a 15-year-old, Kewell flew to England and was able to stay with relatives as he quickly made an impact at Elland Road, making his first-team debut at the age of just 16. But while voices behind the scenes attempted to persuade him to pledge his allegiance to his adopted home, Kewell refused to budge. "I was born and bred in Australia and I've always wanted to wear the green and gold," he said. "The thought of playing for England never crossed my mind. There was never any doubt: my country is Australia."

As for Ryan Giggs – another player often thought to have been eligible for England – the Welshman never had the option of following that path, having been born in Cardiff to Welsh parents, and then only moving to the Manchester area when he was seven. He may have captained England schoolboys (under the surname Wilson), but as Mark Wylie of the Manchester United museum explained: "That was due to residence. Plenty of Scots have played for England schools. It just depends on where you go to school."

"Can you tell when the dug-out was invented?"

Aberdeen were the beneficiaries of the first ever dug-out, at Pittodrie in the 1920s. "Apparently the Dons' trainer, Donald Colman, was a boxing and dancing enthusiast obsessed with players' footwork," explains Simon Inglis in his excellent book, Football Grounds of Great Britain. "Because he also made meticulous notes during games, he needed a dry notebook. Thus he had built a sunken, covered area by the touchline, soon termed the 'dug-out'. A few years later

Everton visited, liked the idea and built one at Goodison, and it was not long before every ground had one."

"Who are the nine individuals to have won English football's top-flight league title as both a player and a manager?"

Having delved deep into the archive we have our nine, opening up with Ted Drake, who collected two championships with Arsenal in 1934-35, and 1937-38. As a striker, Drake terrorised defences even more than Thierry Henry, cracking in 42 goals (still a club record) during the Gunners' charge to the second of those crowns. He even managed to score all seven goals in the 7-1 trouncing of Aston Villa that season (it could have been eight had he not been denied by the crossbar). Some serious va-va-voom, there. In 1952, Drake was appointed manager at Chelsea, who were fighting against relegation at the time. "Ted forecast that it would take three years before we started winning 'pots and pans' and he was spot-on," recalled his captain, Roy Bentley. That 1954-55 success would remain Chelsea's last championship until the Roman Abramovich era, when the drought was ended half a century later.

The year after Drake won his final title as a player, Joe Mercer achieved on-field glory with Everton, before repeating the trick at Arsenal in both 1947-48 and 1952-53. He went on to bring the first division title to Manchester City, the last of their two successes, in 1967-68.

Next up is the legendary Liverpool figurehead Bob Paisley, who secured a league winners' medal at Anfield in 1946-47. But it was as manager that he is best remembered, leading the Reds to six league titles between 1976 and 1983. It could have all been so different had he followed his intended path of leaving the club to set up a fruit and veg business. The club persuaded him to stay on in a coaching capacity in 1954, a decision that would finally bear its own fruit more than 20 years later.

Similarly feted at White Hart Lane, Bill Nicholson also achieved the player-manager double as part of the 1950-51 league-winning team, alongside Alf Ramsey, before managing the double-winners of 1960-61. Ramsey himself is another high-profile name on our exalted list, having gone on to glory in charge of Ipswich in 1961-62. Dave Mackay also played in Nicholson's 1960-61 vintage and he followed this up by managing Derby County in their 1974-75 championship campaign.

Ten years later, Howard Kendall added himself to the list, securing the first of two titles in charge of Everton, the second coming in 1986-87. He had, of course, already tasted league success as a player at Goodison back in 1969-70. Across Stanley Park, Kenny Dalglish also matched this feat, albeit as a player-manager in 1985-86, to go with his five earlier titles as a Liverpool player. Further managerial titles came in 1987-88 and 1989-90, before he took Jack Walker's millions and used them wisely enough to edge Blackburn Rovers past the Premiership winning post in 1994-95.

That leaves just George Graham, the last man to attain this venerable double. Having collected the first division title with Arsenal in 1970-71, he eventually left the club, worked part-time as a barman, before returning to win the league as manager on that famous June 1989 evening at Anfield, adding the 1990-91 league title and the domestic cup double in 1992-93.

"Has there ever been a football manager or players who have attempted to harness psychic abilities and, if so, were there any reports of this being a success?"

Always one to seek an extra edge, the ever-flamboyant Malcolm Allison got in touch with the hypnotist/illusionist Romark (real name Ronald Markham) during his spell as manager at Crystal Palace in the mid-1970s. The pair fell out, however, amid reports of an unpaid bill, and Romark apparently placed a curse on Palace. Then, on the eve of Palace's 1976 FA Cup semi-final against Southampton, Romark contacted Lawrie McMenemy's secretary, Val Gardner, and arranged a meeting with the Saints manager. "I took the coward's way out and agreed to see him," McMenemy wrote in a May 2005 Southern Daily Echo column.

"When he came in, his eyes immediately struck me. He had peripheral vision, both eyes staring in different directions. He surprised everyone by asking for two chairs to be placed in the centre of the room facing away from each other two yards apart, then got an apprentice to put his head on one and heels on the other. When he took the chairs away, the lad stayed suspended in mid-air. I was even asked to sit on the lad's stomach and still he stayed suspended. George Horsfall, our reserve-team trainer, came in shortly afterwards and, after telling him what had happened, he did the trick all over again. He wouldn't tell us how it had been done, but George was born in India and it may well have had something to do with the old Indian rope trick." Ruse or not, it did the trick, Southampton beating Palace 2-0 before going on to upset Manchester United in the final.

Romark's work was not yet done, however. The curse apparently transferred to Allison himself, who went on to manage Manchester City, and on the eve of their 1980 FA Cup third-round tie at Fourth Division Halifax, the Halifax manager George Kirby enlisted Romark's assistance. Speaking in the Lancashire Evening Post, striker John Smith recalled that, two days before the tie, "I'm sat there with this guy called Romark, and he was saying ... 'you will go to sleep now, John Smith, and then you'll overcome the power of Manchester City. You will play the greatest game of your life, John Smith. When I count to three, you'll wake up again'. I was trying not to laugh and I'm thinking, what's all this about? What a load of nonsense." Smith would subsequently lay on the winner for Paul Hendrie in a 2-1 win for the Shaymen. "All the headlines, though, were about that hypnotist," said Smith, "but we beat Manchester City through courage, hard work and belief."

The mysterious Romark would later attempt to prove his powers by driving blindfolded through the streets of Ilford, only for his journey to reach a rather abrupt end after approximately 20 yards when he crashed into the back of a police van. "That van was parked in a place that logic told me it wouldn't be," he claimed. After being imprisoned for embezzling his mother, Romark died of a stroke in 1982.

Another man not shy of self-publicity is Uri Geller, who claims to have used his "miraculous" powers on a number of occasions in football, though not at the behest of any individual in the game. Even during his infamous spell as co-chairman of Exeter City, Geller insisted he would leave the on-field matters to manager John Cornforth. "Whilst I advocate a positive work ethic and optimistic outlook, I will absolutely refrain from using any form of paranormal activity," he told the club's official website in May 2002. The Grecians were relegated to the Conference 12 months later.

Though it's not quite psychic assistance, Bristol Rovers attempted to tap into the art of feng shui in 1999, inviting "experts" Guy de Beaujeu and Patrick Stockhausen to the Memorial Ground in a bid to bring them some luck. "The two men placed a ceramic frog above the entrance, potted plants in the dressing room and a tank of toy fish behind the goal," explained Scott Murray in the Guardian. "It didn't work – Rovers lost their next match 1-0 against

Gillingham – and no wonder, as the pair were filming a hoax TV series called Gatecrasher." However, Rovers nearly had the last, er, merk, as their form picked up and they eventually missed out on the play-offs by a matter of two points. "They obviously knew a lot more than they thought because, since then, we have not stopped winning," noted a club spokesperson.

"Who holds the record for the fastest own goal ever?"

Our instinct was that Steve Bould owned such an honour, having shanked comically past John Lukic just 13 seconds into a league game against Sheffield Wednesday in February 1990. But Pat Kruse, erstwhile Torquay clogger of the seventies, went a full seven seconds better than that. On 3 January 1977, Cambridge United kicked off a league match by lumping the ball straight downfield, where Kruse leapt to head the ball past his goalkeeper. Genius. The goal was timed at six seconds and remains a record in British football.

"Has a goalkeeper ever been caught offside?"

On 4 February 1997, during the dying seconds of an FA Cup fourth-round replay at Wimbledon, Manchester United were trailing 1-0 when Peter Schmeichel embarked on his usual cavalry charge. After a deep corner was headed back into the box by Gary Pallister, Schmeichel directed a spectacular scissors-kick flying into the corner of the net – only to be flagged offside, with two other United players. Wimbledon would hang on and win.

"Has there ever been a deaf professional footballer?"

There have indeed, including one very big name. Though not totally deaf, Arsenal's former record goalscorer, Cliff Bastin, suffered from a severe hearing impairment that prevented his conscription during the second world war. He did serve as an air raid precaution warden during the conflict, stationed on top of the Highbury stadium, despite wildly inaccurate reports to the contrary among Mussolini's fascist press, which claimed that Bastin had been captured during the Battle of Crete.

According to the British Deaf Football website, the likes of Rodney Marsh and Jimmy Case also suffered from hearing problems during their illustrious careers, while there are currently 25 active deaf football clubs competing around Great Britain. Among them is Glasgow Deaf Athletic Football Club, which is the world's oldest deaf football club and, having been founded in 1871, is seven years older than Manchester United.

"Which British football clubs currently have, or have had, Latin words or phrases on their club badges? Can I have translations too?"

There are still a good number of clubs whose badges dabble in the noble (but very dead) language. The Blackburn Rovers motto is *Arte et Labore*, which means "by skill and hard work", while the inscription on Everton's badge reads *Nil Satis Nisi Optimum* and roughly translates as "nothing but the best is good enough". Manchester City's maxim is *Superbia in Proelia*, which as every Latin scholar knows means "pride in battle", and Spurs rejoiced in the SAS-like exhortation *Audere est Facere*, or "to dare is to do", until January 2006, when they dropped the signature from their badge. "It strikes me as a shame to lose it," said Dr Peter Jones, the joint founder of the charity Friends of Classics. "It seems pointless to me and sums up the contempt football clubs have for their fans."

In the lower leagues, Sheffield Wednesday boast of *Consilio et Animis* – which means "by wisdom and courage"; Barnsley offer *Spectamur Agendo* ("let us be judged by our actions"); Tranmere Rovers' old crest bears the legend *Ubi Fides ibi Lux et Robur*, or "where there is faith there is light and strength" and Bury's decrees *Vincit Omnia Industria* – "hard work conquers all".

North of the border, Kilmarnock offer the simple yet classy *Confidemus* ("we trust") and Elgin City win the comedy rosette for their *Sic Itur Ad Astra* ("thus do we reach the stars"). But the prize for non-pretentiousness goes to Queen's Park, who meekly suggest *Ludere Causa Ludendi*, which means "to play for the sake of playing".

"Can you settle an office dispute? During England's goalless draw with Colombia in September 1995, had the referee already blown for offside when René Higuita made his infamous scorpion save?"

Jamie Redknapp's lob was heading towards goal in the 22nd minute of a tedious Wembley stalemate when Higuita dived underneath the ball and performed his astonishing airborne back-flick to clear the ball away. The Scorpion Kick was born and producers of zany sporting highlights shows were rubbing their hands with glee. And soon it was forgotten that the goal wouldn't have counted anyway because the linesman's flag was up for offside. Higuita, however, countered that he was not aware of it. In 2008, *El Loco* was awarded the Best Football Trick Ever award by footy-boots.com and explained how the Scorpion came about: "I was shooting a Colombian soft drink TV commercial with some kids. One of the kids chipped the ball over me and I reacted with the Scorpion move. Luckily, they were recording at the time and the Scorpion trick ended up on the commercial. Five years later, and after the Scorpion had been on the commercial time and again, I'd get loads of requests from fans and people around the world asking me to perform [it]. So I decided to do the Scorpion live to the world."

"Have any high-profile matches attracted uproar due to their notorious nature?"

Perhaps the most tarnished game of all took place during the 1982 World Cup in Spain, when West Germany and Austria met in the final match of Group B. The Teutonic neighbours were well aware that a 1-0 win for the Germans would ensure that both sides would qualify for the next round at the expense of Algeria. Sure enough, a Horst Hrubesch goal gave West Germany the lead after only 10 minutes, at which point the game ground to a virtual halt.

Despite catcalls and chants of "Algeria! Algeria!" from the crowd and the sight of one German fan even burning the national flag in disgust, the pat-a-cake continued for a full 80 minutes, at which point both sides walked off congratulating themselves on a job well done. Jupp Derwall, the West Germany coach defended his team, citing their "right to be careful in this game". Reasonably enough, Algeria protested to Fifa, the president of their FA Benali Sekkal branding the match "scandalous and immoral", but to no avail. Four years later, in Mexico, Fifa ensured that the last round of matches in the first round took place concurrently.

A near-scandal of a South American flavour had taken place at the 1978 World Cup in Argentina, where the hosts, under serious pressure from the ruling military junta, needed to beat Peru by four goals in the last of the second-round group matches if they were to pip Brazil to a place in the final. Amid allegations of match-fixing and a $50m junta-paid slush fund for the Peruvian authorities – all of which remain unproven to this day – Argentina thumped Peru 6-0 to squeeze out their arch-rivals and reach the final, where two goals from Mario Kempes helped see off Holland 3-1.

And there was also a whiff of suspicion about Spain's path to the finals of the 1984 European Championship in France. Having lost 2-1 in an earlier qualification game to Holland, the Spanish went into their final match needing to beat Malta by 11 clear goals, a feat that appeared unlikely when they went in at half-time with a tenuous 3-1 lead. But, suddenly in the second half, the floodgates opened and Spain got the nine goals they needed to win 12-1 and qualify. One of the country's most venerable sports writers, Henry Brincat, wrote in the Times of Malta that "never in the history of Maltese soccer have we ever touched rock bottom", while magistrate Dennis Montebello headed up an inquiry into the defeat, although it failed to draw any major conclusions.

"People will always spread rumours about a public figure," the 12-times beaten goalkeeper John Bonello told Malta Today in 2006. "But the inquiry wasn't just about me. The whole team was responsible for the result." Bonello went on to head a possibly ill-advised advertising campaign for Amstel in Spain, where he had developed folk hero status, and inevitably faced much criticism in Malta for doing so. "Whoever thinks it is humiliating to do such an advert is just plain ignorant," Bonello insisted. "They chose me as a sportsman, not because of the game."

Suffice to say, there were few neutrals weeping for Spain when they lost 2-0 in the final to France.

"Their flag is green, white and red, so why do Italy play in blue?"

Blue is the colour of Savoia which, as you may or may not know, was the ruling house of Italy from 1861 to 1946. Until the end of the second world war, the country's flag always had the Savoy coat of arms on it. Only since the family was overthrown and the Italian Republic was established post-war has the plain tricolor been adopted as the national flag, while the blue shirts of the Azzurri continue to pay tribute to the Italian monarchy to this day.

"With the prospect of two players of English descent – Aaron Hunt and Lewis Holtby – playing for Germany at the 2010 World Cup, I was wondering if there were any Englishmen who had represented another major international team?"

The answer is a lot more than you might think and, therefore, we have excluded "Englishmen" (ie born in England or have at least one English parent) who have represented Scotland, Northern Ireland, Wales or the Republic of Ireland. To start us off, there is Giuseppe

Wilson, born plain old Joseph Wilson in Darlington in 1945, who was capped three times by Italy in 1974. His father Dennis had met his Italian mother Lina d'Francesca in Italy while serving in the British Army during the second world war, and when he was six months old, the family moved to Naples, where he would begin his career before moving to Lazio. Of his three caps, he made one substitute appearance against Poland in the 1974 World Cup.

Even though England failed to reach the 1974 finals, Wilson was not the only Englishman at that World Cup. In fact, not even the only Englishman named Wilson at that World Cup either. The Australia captain, Peter Wilson, was also born in the north east (Felling, County Durham, in 1947) and had only emigrated down under in 1969. He would eventually win 65 caps for his adopted country. Also at the 1974 World Cup and in the same group as Italy, but playing for Argentina, was Carlos Alberto Babington. Born in 1949 to an English father and known in Argentina as *El Inglés* (the Englishman), Babington won 13 international caps as a striker, scoring two goals.

Babington is one of a number of Britons (or players with British ancestors) that have played for South American countries. Among their number are Sidney Pullen, born in Southampton in 1895 and believed to be the only foreigner to have ever played for Brazil. When his father was transferred to a job in Rio de Janeiro and his family emigrated, Pullen subsequently played for Paysandu, Flamengo and also Brazil. Harry Hayes (aka Juán Enrique Hayes) won 21 caps for Argentina between 1910 and 1919, scoring eight goals, after being born in Rosario to English parents, and Alfredo Peel Yates also won four caps for the country in 1911 and is listed as Argentina's only English-born international.

Alberto Pedro Spencer made the same number of international appearances for Uruguay, but also made 11 for Ecuador, all between 1959 and 1972. Spencer was born in Ecuador in 1937, the son of a British Jamaican and was eventually recognised for his illustrious career when named as the 20th greatest South American player of the 20th century by the International Federation of Football History and Statistics.

However, the greatest British footballing family in South American history was the Browns. James and Mary Brown emigrated to Argentina from Scotland aboard the ship Symmetry in August 1825 and ultimately six of their grandchildren would later play for the national team. Jorge Gibson Brown (1880-1936), known as *El Patriarcho*, played in Argentina's first ever game and won 23 caps in all, scoring four times. Four of Jorge's brothers also played for Argentina: Carlos Carr Brown won two caps in 1903 and 1905; Ernesto Alejandro Brown won 12 caps and scored once between 1902 and 1912; Alfredo Carrow Brown won nine caps (four goals); and Eliseo Brown won 10 caps (six goals), both between 1906 and 1911. The brothers had a cousin who would also play for Argentina, Juan Domingo Brown, who collected 36 caps and two goals between 1906 and 1916, while two other cousins – Diego and Tomás – were also footballers. Incidentally, another direct descendent of James and Mary scored in the 1986 World Cup final – José Luis Brown scored the opener in the 3-2 win over West Germany.

In fact, team line-ups for internationals between South American countries had a very British feel to them in the early 20th century, reflecting the massive influence of expats in the development of the game in the continent. In 1910, when Argentina beat Chile 5-1 in the first unofficial Copa América, the Argentina team included Carlos Wilson, Jorge Brown, Juan Domingo Brown, Arturo Jacobs, Ernesto Brown and Harry Hayes, while Chile fielded Luis Gibson, EF Ashe, J MacWilliams, Henry Allen, Joe Robson, Colin Campbell, Juan Hamilton, Heriberto Sturgess and JP Davidson.

Back in Europe, Alfred "Fred" Aston was capped on 31 occasions by France and played in both the 1934 and 1938 World Cups. He was born in France in 1912 to an English father and French mother, and shone during two spells for club side Red Star FC after beginning his working life as an apprentice jockey at Chantilly. But even Aston was not the first Englishman to play in the World Cup finals. That honour belonged to George Moorhouse, a Liverpudlian who represented the United States in both the 1930 and 1934 finals (where he captained the side). Moorhouse had been born in Liverpool in May 1901 and, after serving with the Merchant Navy during the first world war, played twice for Tranmere before emigrating to Canada in 1923 and later moving to the US. The USA also had five more players born in Scotland who played in the 1930 World

Cup finals – Bart McGhee, Andy Auld, Jim Brown, Jimmy Gallagher and Alec Wood.

More recently, Muzzy Izzet was born in Mile End, London, to a Turkish Cypriot father and an English mother, before going on to represent Turkey on eight occasions (including the 2002 World Cup), while fellow east-ender Colin Kazim-Richards also chose to represent Turkey through his mother's Turkish Cypriot roots. "In England, people don't see me as Turkish," the former Bury forward told the Observer in 2008. "Like when police stop me, it's not because I'm Turkish, it's because I'm black."

The Singapore international, Daniel Bennett, was born in Great Yarmouth in January 1978, but moved out to Asia with his family when he was just two. After studying at Loughborough University and playing for two spells with Wrexham, Bennett returned to Singapore, where he is closing in on a century of caps. And finally, Simone Perrotta, the World Cup-winning Italy midfielder, spent the first six years of his life in Ashton-under-Lyne (birthplace of Sir Geoff Hurst), until his parents Francesco and Anna Maria left their jobs where they helped run the Yates' Wine Lodge in the town and moved home to Cosenza. "I have a few memories of Ashton, but they are just flashes," admitted Perotta, whose mother insists that Simone will finish his career back in England. "He is proud to be Italian, but I know he has a little part of him that is English as well," she said.

"Are there any league players who can boast the feat of an own-goal hat-trick in one game?"

Amazingly, there is. During Anderlecht's 4-2 win over Germinal Ekeren in a 1995-96 Belgian Premier League match, three of their goals were scored by the hapless Staf van den Buys. Many English players have done their best to match the feat: Sunderland managed three in eight minutes at home to Charlton in February 2003 – but Michael Proctor could only bag two of them in a 3-1 loss. Jamie Carragher also struck twice in Liverpool's 3-2 defeat by Manchester United in September 1999. And Aston Villa's Chris Nicholl scored all four goals in a 2-2 draw against Leicester in March 1976.

"I'm fairly sure that, a few years ago, Liam Daish got sent off when a fan threw a bugle on the pitch and he picked it up and played a tune on it. Can anyone else confirm this?"

The former Republic of Ireland international did indeed incur the referee's wrath for his particularly poor Louis Armstrong impression – only he saw yellow, not red. Still, the crazy caution was enough for Daish to be suspended for two matches. The incident took place during Birmingham City's 4-0 win over Chester City in December 1994, when Daish – the Blues' skipper – was celebrating the fourth goal of the game. In the ensuing revelry, a fan tossed a toy trumpet on to the pitch, which Daish proceeded to play. Although he avoided a dismissal, the booking took his disciplinary points tally to 41 and a resulting ban. As for manager Barry Fry's reaction? "I know the referee has directives to adhere to, but to get banned through being booked for that seems a bit harsh," he parped.

"Which club has broken the most records in a single season?"

It is difficult to look beyond the remarkable (in so many bad ways) 1965-66 Bundesliga campaign of Tasmania Berlin. Having only finished third in the Regionalliga Berlin, Tasmania were preparing for another year in the division when Hertha Berlin were found guilty of illicit player payments and demoted. The German football authorities, which had only just expanded the Bundesliga to 18 teams, desperately needed West Berlin to have a top-flight team, leaving Tasmania as the lucky beneficiaries, albeit with just two weeks' notice (When Saturday Comes explains that "Radio Luxembourg had to broadcast an urgent appeal to Tasmania's players to return to Berlin from their holidays").

Life started well when 81,000 fans packed into the Olympiastadion to watch an opening 3-1 victory against Karlsruhe, though they would only win one more game all season, a 2-1 success in the penultimate match against Neunkirchen. In between, Tasmania were busy setting an unlucky single-season 13 records in becoming the worst ever team in top-flight German history. For the purists among you, the list in full: fewest wins of all time (two); fewest draws of all time (four); most losses of all time (28); least goals for (15); most goals against (108); smallest points total (eight); longest winless streak ever (31 games, between August 1965 and May 1966); longest losing streak ever (10 games, equalled in 1998 by Arminia Bielefeld); longest goal drought ever (831 minutes, since surpassed by Saarbrücken and Cologne); smallest average attendance in Bundesliga history; smallest ever Bundesliga crowd (827); biggest home defeat (9-0 to Meidericher SV) and the lowest number of goals ever scored by a team's top scorer (four – Wulf-Ingo Usbeck).

"Which English counties are not represented in the Premier/Football League?"

Well, with 48 counties (according to the current county system as used by your local postie) and 92 clubs to choose from, you would have thought it would only be fair for every county to have at least one. But as we all know, life is never fair and it makes no exceptions for the poor souls of Cornwall, for example, who invariably have to make a trip across the River Tamar into next-door Devon if they want to splash their hard-earned cash on the excesses of Plymouth Argyle. And it is the south-west that has suffered more than most – it took promotions for Yeovil

Town (2002-03) and Cheltenham Town (1998-99) to bring League football to Somerset and Gloucester, respectively.

Other counties lacking the beauty of a concrete terrace and a decent pie on a Saturday, at the time of writing before the end of the 2009-10 season, are Surrey (though the twinning arrangement with the red half of Manchester eases the pain), Bedfordshire, Oxfordshire, West Sussex, the Isle of Wight, Shropshire, Worcestershire, Warwickshire and Northumberland. However, residents of Northumberland can take solace in the thrills and spills of Scottish league football, courtesy of Berwick Rangers.

"Have any teams ever finished their domestic seasons with a goal difference of +100 or better?"

Beyond the amateur game, such a blend of striking prowess and defensive prudence is a combination so rare that we were only able to uncover five examples in four countries. Germany is the only country in which this remarkable feat has been achieved twice: in the 1936-37 Gauliga Westfalen season, Schalke scored 140 times on their way to a final goal differential of +119; this was quickly followed in the 1942-43 Gauliga Sachsen season by Dresdner SC, whose players displayed an uncanny level of concentration in and around the penalty box, putting 152 goals past flailing opposition keepers and conceding just 16, leaving them with a difference of +136 and not a single dropped point throughout the entire season.

More recently, in the further reaches of Macedonia, FK Vardar appeared to spend the whole of the 1992-93 campaign running rings around their rivals to score an impressive 119 times and finish with a goal difference of +103. Vardar's achievement is matched by Barry Town's 1997-98 season in the League of Wales, when the team went 38 games unbeaten (33 wins), scoring 134 times and conceding 31. However, the principals of the penalty box are Hungarian team MTK Budapest, who, in 1917-18, fired 147 goals past their league opponents, who we can only assume stood gaping-mouthed and motionless for the best part of 90 minutes every week – an assumption bolstered by the fact that they let in only 10 to leave themselves 137 goals to the good.

"In 2001-02, Valencia won the Spanish title scoring only 51 goals in 38 games, an average of just 1.34 goals per game. Have any other championship-winning teams managed a lower average?"

Of course they have and – surprise, surprise – you don't have to look much further than Serie A for textbook examples. Italian football is full of goal-shy scudetto winners. One thinks of Bologna in 1935-36, who scored 39 goals in 30 games (at an average of 1.30 per game) or the Fiorentina side of 1968-69 (38 goals in 30 games at an average of 1.27). But none comes close to matching the feat of Milan in 1993-94.

They scored a miserable 36 goals in 34 matches (1.06 per game), but conceded just 15, meaning that their regular followers would have seen exactly 1.5 goals every game. Or one per hour. Perhaps that is not too surprising – after all, the Milan defence was strong-armed by the likes of Franco Baresi, Alessandro Costacurta and Paolo Maldini (with Marcel Desailly sweeping up in midfield), while their attack was blunted by the career-ending injury to Marco van Basten. Still, they were good enough going forward to destroy Barcelona 4-0 in the European Cup final.

You may be wondering about Helenio Herrera's famous Inter side of the mid-1960s. Well, the team that pioneered catenaccio was not as negative as history remembers them, scoring an average of 2.00 goals a game in their scudetto win of 1964-65 and 2.06 per match in their 1965-66 triumph.

As for the title of "most boring league champions ever", Swedish team AIK Stockholm "bested" Milan's mark as they won the Allsvenskan by scoring a frankly pathetic 25 times in 26 games, just 0.96 goals per game. Each of the other 13 teams in the division scored more, including relegated pair Östers IF and BK Häcken.

"Which club has gone through the most managers in a single season?"

While QPR have made a valiant effort during 2009-10, playing under Jim Magilton, Steve Gallen and Marc

Bicham (caretakers), Paul Hart, Mick Harford (caretaker) and Neil Warnock, it will probably come as little surprise that the record holders are the farcically-run club otherwise known as Atlético Madrid. When someone once wisecracked that there are more than three million unemployed in Spain and at least half of them are former Atlético managers, they were not too far from the truth.

At the heart of it all was their infamous jailbird president Jesús Gil, a maverick who bore more than a passing resemblance to the love child of Happy Days' Howard Cunningham and Al Delvecchio. His approach to hiring and firing saw 20 different managers at the Vicente Calderón in the first six years of his reign from 1987 (including 95 days of Ron Atkinson in 1988), while a grand total of 39 coaches went through his revolving door in 17 years. "Appointing a coach means no more to me than ordering a glass of sherry," he once said. "I don't care if I have to try 100 glasses a year to find the right one." One man who did care was the Brazilian Joaquín Peiró who, as legend has it, was jettisoned before the 1990-91 season had even begun because Gil did not like the look of him in the official team photograph.

Come 1993-94, Atlético were headed by six different managers. First through the doors was Jair Pereira, only appointed that summer, who was sacked in October. Cacho Heredia and Emilio Cruz then lasted two months each; José Romero one month; Santos Ovejero arrived in March and left in ... you guessed it, March. And finally Jorge d'Alessandro managed to steer Atlético through to the end of the season, finishing 12th ... he was gone soon after. Gil died in 2004, but the club remains in the shambolic state in which he left it.

"After reading about Scotland's inauspicious 1978 World Cup campaign, I got to wondering about their coach Ally MacLeod. When he claimed that 'my name is Ally MacLeod and I am a born winner', did he have any basis for this statement?"

Ally MacLeod was born in Glasgow on 26 February 1931, and judging by his record as a player and a manager, it's a fair bet that he did not come out with the word "winner" stamped across his forehead. After a time on the field which included spells at Third Lanark, St Mirren, Blackburn Rovers, Hibernian and Ayr United (major honours: zero), MacLeod embarked on a managerial career that can only be described as a one-man roadshow of broken promises and shattered dreams.

On being appointed manager (and commercial manager) at Ayr in 1966, he took the team he inherited – Second Division champions that had scored the best part of 90 goals the previous year – and sadly led them back whence they had came within a season. Admittedly, better days followed. In 1969, Ayr returned to the top flight, where the club enjoyed a golden age, finishing in the top seven in 1973, 1974 and 1975. In the process, MacLeod won Ayr's Citizen of the Year Award for 1973, while the club set their attendance record: a 2-1 win over Rangers, watched by 25,225.

More success followed. In 1975, MacLeod – who summed up his philosophy as "if the manager keeps saying we'll win, we'll win, we'll win, then eventually the players will believe it" – moved to Aberdeen, where he led the Dons to a League Cup triumph and the Premier League runners-up spot. Small wonder, then, that in May 1977, the Scottish FA came knocking. Their previous manager, Willie Ormond, had performed satisfactorily during his four-year tenure, but with player indiscipline growing, the SFA wanted a more forceful and charismatic leader. Step forward Ally MacLeod, who brusquely introduced himself to the squad and the press with the immortal "born winner" line in question.

Within a year, it had all gone disastrously wrong. Scotland's World Cup campaign started on a high, MacLeod declaring to the world that he would be back with "at least a medal", to a background of maniacally happy fans chanting along to "We're on the way wi' Ally's Army". But two frankly embarrassing performances against Peru and Iran, a drugs scandal involving Willie Johnston and a too-little-too-late win over Holland later, the squad was back home. "I am a very good manager who just happened to have a few disastrous days, once upon a time, in Argentina," he offered poetically in his 1979 autobiography, the Ally MacLeod Story.

MacLeod's fate was a series of jobs (at Motherwell, Airdrie, Ayr and Queen of the South) throughout the

80s, and his return to Somerset Park between 1986 and 1989 is still fondly remembered in Ayr, largely because he kept them in the Scottish Football League. He died after suffering from Alzheimer's, aged 72 in 2004. "I heard all the jokes about how that must have been a good thing for him because finally he could forget about Argentina," his widow Faye told Scotland on Sunday in 2008. "But the truth is he never forgot."

"Which player has gone the longest without losing with his country?"

Everyone has got a long way to go to beat Garrincha in the longest-winning period stakes, the brilliant Brazilian winger playing in 50 internationals and winning two World Cups in the process. Eleven years, 43 wins, six draws and 12 goals after he made his debut at the Maracana against Chile in 1955, Garrincha eventually lost his 50th and final Brazil game, against Hungary at the 1966 World Cup.

"Monaco's 8-3 trouncing of Deportivo: the biggest ever in Europe's premier competition or not?"

Admittedly, the Dado Prso-inspired beat-down in November 2003 was arguably the most impressive in the history of the European Cup since Real Madrid beat Eintracht Frankfurt 7-3 in the perpetually-recalled 1960 final at Hampden Park. This was because Depor were third in La Liga at the time and therefore good, unlike some of the victims you will read about in the following thrashfest.

The previous high score in the Champions League was totted up by Paris St-Germain, who walloped Rosenborg 7-2 in October 2000. (Oddly, the Norwegians themselves had spanked Helsingborg 6-1 only two matches earlier.) Rangers also won a Champions League game 7-2, Ally McCoist running riot against Alania Vladikavkaz of Russia in August 1996, but that was in qualifying so does not count. (In any case, even if it did, both FC Porto and Dinamo Kyiv have bested it by skelping poor Barry Town of Wales 8-0 – in July 2001 and July 1998, respectively – a feat matched by Poles Widzew Lodz against Neftchi Baku of Azerbaijan in July 1997.)

For the record, the biggest score by any British team in the group stages was posted by Liverpool, who crashed eight past Besiktas in November 2007. However, much as Uefa and Sky would like to convince us otherwise, the tournament did not begin in the Champions League era. The biggest British European Cup wins of all time were posted by Leeds United in November 1969, who beat Lyn Oslo 10-0 (and won the second leg 6-0 in Norway), and Ipswich, who whacked Malta's Floriana in a similar double-digit style at Portman Road in September 1962. In hot pursuit are Liverpool: on their way to the 1981 title, they won 10-1 against OPS of Finland. There's also a 10-0 for Manchester United against Anderlecht, in September

1956, at Maine Road while the blitz-damaged Old Trafford was being repaired, but that does not count. Preliminaries. Sorry.

(While we're at it, Leeds's 16-goal romp was not the biggest two-leg battering in the tournament's history; Benfica crushed Stade Dudelange of Luxembourg 8-0 and 10-0 in September/October 1965.)

Back to more high scores. Leeds, Liverpool, Ipswich and Benfica are not the only clubs to have hit 10 at Europe's top table: Anderlecht won at Valkeakosken Haka of Finland 10-1 in September 1966, while Ajax posted a 10-0 demolition of Omonia Nicosia in October 1979. In fact, Ajax were rampant that season, twice belabouring HJK Helsinki 8-1 in the first round, scoring four without reply in the return against a totally dispirited Omonia in the second, and beating Strasbourg 4-0 in the last eight. That is as good as it got: they lost 2-1 on aggregate against eventual champions Nottingham Forest in the semi-final.

But there are two teams that can beat even the magic 10. In October 1973, Dudu Georgescu and Radu Nunweiller shared eight goals between them as Dinamo Bucharest of Romania followed up a 1-0 first-round, first-leg victory with an 11-0 pasting of Northern Ireland side Crusaders, the biggest-ever margin of victory in the competition. However, the title of top tormentors goes to Feyenoord, who, en route to picking up the trophy in 1970, put 12 past KR of Reykjavik, conceding a mere two at the other end. The second leg was an anticlimactic 4-0 win. Remember:

in Iceland, KR of Reykjavik were that year referred to as "champions".

As for Europe's two other main competitions, Ajax hold the Uefa Cup single-game record after a 14-0 spanking of Red Boys Differdange of Luxembourg (it had been goalless in the first leg) in October 1984, while Feyenoord's 21-0 two-leg spanking of US Rumelange (again of Luxembourg) in 1972 is enough for the aggregate best. Chelsea matched this mark in their 1971 Cup Winners' Cup first-round destruction of Jeunesse Hautcharage (hmm, of Luxembourg), but the biggest single European win belongs to Sporting Lisbon, who won 16-1 (Knowledge vidiprinter – SIXTEEN) against Cypriots Apoel Nicosia in the first leg of their 1963 second-round tie. The 2-0 return leg was, in all fairness, something of a letdown.

"Has the 1986 England World Cup squad got the worst managerial record ever?"

In a word, yes. The 1986 squad has proven that it had about as much savvy in the world of football management as a chicken balti pie. Of the 22-man squad, a dozen went on to "enjoy" post-playing careers of varying, though consistently short, length.

Peter Shilton, goalkeeper extraordinaire, manager non-descript, lasted just three years at Plymouth Argyle, in which time he all-but-ruined the club and left a very bitter taste in the mouths of supporters. His long-standing gambling habit effectively put an end to his managerial career, while the £7,000 he borrowed (and then failed to repay) from his assistant manager at Home Park, John McGovern, effectively ended their friendship that had built from their Nottingham Forest days.

And he was one of the stayers, with most of this duff lot lasting around the 12-month mark. Kenny Sansom was pretty feeble as Glenn Roeder's assistant at Watford; Mark Hateley took just over one season to push Hull City to the brink of non-league football before he was given his marching orders; and Chris Waddle's season at Burnley also ended up with the Clarets touching relegation cloth. Kerry Dixon put in a year at Doncaster Rovers and bothered Letchworth Town for a bit, before stints with Boreham Wood, Hitchin Town and Dunstable.

Ray Wilkins was pleased to get the nod from Fulham when he was sacked by QPR after a year – but lightning really can strike in the same place twice and he was out on his ear again after another 12-month flailing. Following assistant roles with Millwall and the England Under-21s, Wilkins replaced Steve Clarke as Chelsea's first-team coach in September 2008, where he has remained ever since.

Then there are the managers from this shabby group that were given the boot even before they had managed to pay the removal men and unpack the winter wardrobe. Take a bow, John Barnes, who lasted eight months at Celtic before a 3-1 Scottish Cup defeat at home to Inverness Caledonian Thistle put the rubber stamp on his P45. A dodgy spell as a Channel Five football host followed, before a six-month spell in charge of Jamaica acted as the prelude to another forgettable four months as the Tranmere Rovers boss. Alongside assistant Jason McAteer, the pair won three of their first 14 games before being turfed out on their ears.

Terry Butcher, having put in a year at Coventry, was sacked just three months into the 1993-94 season by Sunderland, by which time he had managed to settle them nicely into 22nd, following this up with other unremarkable spells with Sydney FC, Brentford (where he won five of 23 before being axed) and Inverness CT, where he failed to prevent their relegation from the SPL in 2009.

The less said about the managerial career of Bryan Robson the better, though Glenn Hoddle did succeed with Swindon and Chelsea, before his elevation to England manager and subsequent infamous pre-sacking claim that "you and I have been physically given two hands and two legs and half-decent brains. Some people have not been born like that for a reason. The karma is working from another lifetime." Failures at Southampton, Tottenham and Wolves followed. Peter Reid is arguably the most consistent of the bunch, guiding Sunderland into the top-flight on two occasions, and Manchester City to fifth place in the First Division in back-to-back seasons, but he was eventually sacked from both jobs, before uninspired stints with Leeds United and Coventry City. His latest role is as assistant with Stoke City.

But when it comes to Terry Fenwick, it appears like there is no end to the curse of the Hand of God. After replacing Jim Smith in August 1995, Fenwick remained at Fratton Park (for a time under chairman Terry Venables) until January 1998, by which point they had won just 43 of 131 games in his tenure, concluding with an 11-game winless streak that left them rooted to the foot of the First Division, and managed to alienate the vast majority of the club's fans. Writing in When Saturday Comes in 2001, Pompey fan Steve Morgan explained how he "had never liked Fenwick – I found it impossible to forget that Bobby Robson thought he was an arsehole because he'd said going away with England was boring … by God, he was unlovable." After spells in non-league football and in Trinidad & Tobago, Fenwick was then handed the reins at Northampton Town in 2003 (upon which the Cobblers' internet message boards were filled with sympathy from Portsmouth supporters), where he slogged for seven whole games and 49 days before he received his marching orders. His latest post has been as the head coach of Trinidad & Tobago side San Juan Jabloteh.

"Is it true that the goalkeeper Steve Ogrizovic was once arrested on spying charges in Kazakhstan?"

Not quite, is the honest answer. Back in January 2003, an internet plea on petitiononline.com claimed that the former Coventry City goalkeeper had been on a round-the-world trip to raise funds for charity when he had accidentally "trespassed on to Kazakhstani private military land" and was being held on suspicion of being a spy. "Here is our petition to Tony Blair and the Kazakhstani government demanding the release of footballing legend Steve Ogrizovic and protesting his innocence," began the Free Steve Ogrizovic Appeal. "Please sign this petition and help bring forward the release of Steve Ogrizovic."

More than 250 Sky Blues fans flocked to the site and posted supportive messages, only for Ogrizovic to soon be tracked down at the club's Ryton training ground, where he was working as the club's academy director. "This is a complete hoax," he told the Coventry Evening Telegraph. "I haven't a clue where it has come from. I am told that only 57 people signed the petition to get me back so I don't think that would carry much weight with Tony Blair. The first I heard about it was when a journalist from the Guardian rang me and asked what I was doing answering the phone when I should have been locked away in a prison cell in Kazakhstan. The first thing I did was go to an atlas and have a look where it is."

The Guardian added that "not all who signed the petition were supportive of Ogrizovic, however. 'Lock him up for life,' wrote someone claiming to be the keeper's brother. 'I've forever been in the shadows of the big ugly bastard. Cutting off his hands would be ideal because these are the main cause for his success.'"

"Footballers are always hitting the headlines after landing in court on driving or assault charges, but has a professional footballer ever done anything really bad like murder?"

We did uncover quite a few criminal records in the world of football, and not just those released in the run-ups to FA Cup finals. During his teenage playing days with Ajax, Patrick Kluivert was found guilty of causing death by dangerous driving in September 1995. Found to be speeding at approximately 55mph in a 35mph when his red BMW Cabriolet smashed into the side of 56-year-old father of two Marten Putman's Ford Orion in Amsterdam, Kluivert was sentenced to 240 hours of community service. "Something inside me is broken, I can never be fully happy again," Kluivert told Voetbal International magazine. "The child in me has been killed." After the sentencing, Putman's widow said: "He has ruined my life, but it is very important for me he was found guilty. It was a soft sentence, but that was normal for the Netherlands."

The West Brom striker Lee Hughes was also found guilty of causing death by dangerous driving and was jailed for six years in August 2004 after his Mercedes was involved in a crash near his West Midlands home that killed Douglas Graham, a passenger in the other car involved. Hughes fled the scene (Judge Christopher Hodson declared that "I am quite satisfied that in running away you were thinking only of yourself and you were attempting to avoid the legal consequences of driving having consumed alcohol. You clearly believed that if you had been breathalysed, then you would have been over the limit.") and did not hand himself in for a further 34 hours. West Brom sacked him following his conviction, but barely three years into his sentence, Hughes was released from Featherstone prison, whereby he joined Oldham Athletic (at his press conference unveiling, Hughes admitted "I know that 'sorry' isn't good enough"), before moving to Notts County in 2009.

Another tragedy was caused by the Plymouth Argyle goalkeeper Luke McCormick, who in the summer of 2008, fell asleep at the wheel while being twice over the drink-drive limit and crashed his Range Rover into the back of another vehicle on the M6, killing two young brothers, 10-year-old Arron and Ben Peak, eight, in the car. In September of that year, McCormick admitted causing death by dangerous driving and being over the limit, and was jailed for seven years and four months, though he will be eligible for parole at the start of 2012. "He will restart his life when he is still a young man," said the victims' mother Amanda. "Our sons will never experience the things Luke has had."

Best known for the colourful barnets he sported while doing his bit to keep Bradford City in the Premiership at the turn of the millennium, Jamie Lawrence had been sentenced to four years in prison for his part in an armed robbery earlier in a life littered with criminal convictions for theft and assaults. "Being honest, most of my crimes were against people like myself – never against women or old people – and so I thought they deserved what they got," he told the Jamaica Football Federation website. After being sent to the Isle of Wight, Lawrence played for the prison team, before being picked up by local outfit Cowes Sports. After being released 26 months into his sentence, Lawrence was offered a trial (of the football variety) by Sunderland, and his career went from there. "When I am finished, I'd like to work in the community with young people. I'd like to use my experience to show them that, if you get into trouble as a young person, your life is not necessarily over."

The much-travelled former Wales international Mickey Thomas, who spent much of his career with Wrexham and Manchester United, did 18 months of time at Her Majesty's pleasure after being caught distributing counterfeit £10 and £20 notes to trainees at the Racecourse Ground in 1993. "The first place I went, Walton prison in Liverpool, was tough," Thomas told the Observer nine years later, "but after that I had it quite comfortable inside. I made sure I had the best of everything: whatever I wanted to drink, plenty of days at home and, towards the end, I even had my own car." He went on to work the after-dinner circuit, offering up jokes such as "Roy Keane's on 50 grand a week. Mind you, so was I until the police found my printing machine."

Moving on, Ashley Sestanovich, formerly of Sheffield United and a Nike advert body double for Thierry Henry, was jailed for eight years over his role in plotting a robbery that ended in murder. Thomas Fahey was shot dead during a payroll robbery at a Streatham roofing company in June

2005 and while Damien Ennis and Hallroy Reid were found guilty of murder, Sestanovich was convicted of conspiracy to rob, having provided inside information to the pair. "It was particularly satisfying to identify and convict Ashley Sestanovich, without whom the robbery at Fahey Roofing would never have taken place," said Detective Sergeant Steve Kiely after the court case.

Once of Doncaster Rovers and Southend United, David Roche received eight years in jail for his role in a drugs racket after being caught by hidden police cameras selling 5,000 ecstasy tablets, and the former West Ham and Everton midfielder Mark Ward also spent four years (of an eight-year sentence) behind bars for possessing cocaine with an intent to supply. "Someone made me an offer I shouldn't have accepted," he told the Guardian. "They said they'd pay me a weekly wage if I rented a house in my name and handed the keys over to them. I was surviving on income support at the time and foolishly agreed to go along with it. Then the police raided it one day and found £700,000 of cocaine. My name was on the rental agreement. I was arrested." During his time in jail, Ward detailed his life story and released From Right-Wing to B-Wing once he was let out in May 2009. "Nothing can prepare you for what goes on [in prison]," he told the Independent after being freed. "But maybe, in a strange way, having had the life of a professional footballer, that stood me in better stead than some."

Finally, the Tunisian former Fortuna Düsseldorf and Wuppertal player Nizar Trabelsi was jailed for 10 years in 2003 for plotting to blow up the Kleine Brogel Belgian military base used to house US soldiers. During his trial, Trabelsi confessed to meeting al-Qaida leader Osama bin Laden and, according to the BBC, "asked to become a suicide bomber", only to be arrested two days after the 11 September attacks. As a coincidental footnote, Sky News was subsequently forced to offer an on-air apology to Sami Trabelsi, after its news bulletins to report Nizar Trabelsi's imprisonment used the former Tunisia captain's photograph throughout the day. In a statement, Sky said it accepted that Sami Trabelsi had no connection with any terrorist organisation, and recognised that he was a "well respected figure within the Tunisian community".

"Rugby referees are always miked up during games so that television viewers can hear their decisions throughout the game. Has this ever happened in football?"

The 1989 Granada TV programme Out of Order, which called for David Elleray to become the first official to have a microphone attached to him during a match may well have put football's rulers off the idea. The game in question, as recalled by Rob Smyth in the Guardian in 2009, "was a particularly tempestuous affair involving Millwall and Arsenal, in which nearly every word spoken by the players – who had no idea that Elleray was wired for sound – had to be bleeped out. Especially those of Tony Adams, the

Arsenal captain. When Elleray, a Harrow schoolmaster who treated players like pupils, declined to award a goal after Adams had clearly bundled the ball over the line, he lost it, announcing: 'That's my goal!' with a frighteningly pre-pubescent squeak, before calling Elleray a 'fucking cheat'. Elleray booked Adams, prompting a gloriously earnest response of: 'But I'm frustrated!' Elleray called it the most embarrassing experience of his career."

Since then, the Belgian film director Yves Hinant attempted to follow in the footsteps of Zidane: A 21st Century Portrait by making the documentary, Les Arbitres (the Referees), in which the men in the middle are miked up during Euro 2008. Several moments stand out during Massimo Busacca's handling of the Greece v Sweden game, as dialogue between him and his assistants can be heard throughout: when the fourth official warns that a storm is on the way, he snaps: "It's not my problem, shut up." Then, at the conclusion of the game, he tells a beaten Greek player: "We are not gods, we make mistakes." Again, football's agricultural language comes to the fore, especially during Poland's defeat to Austria, when Howard Webb awards a penalty against them in the final minute. The film's working title, Kill the Referee, derived from the subsequent backlash from Poland, including comments from prime minister, Donald Tusk, who said Webb's decision had made him "want to kill".

"When Brazil won the Jules Rimet trophy for a third time in 1970, they were allowed to keep it. If Argentina or Germany triumph again, they would match that achievement, but would Fifa give them the new cup to keep?"

No, is the short answer. All they would receive – like every other World Cup-winning team – would be temporary possession of the trophy for four years and a gold-plated replica. Harsh? Well, perhaps. But Fifa's position is understandable. After all, as stated in the question, it gave away the original trophy to Brazil – a pure gold depiction of the Greek goddess Nike designed by Frenchman Abel Lafleur – only to see it stolen from the Rio de Janeiro headquarters of the Brazilian FA in December 1983 and then believed to have been smelted down by the thieves (of course, the trophy had already been stolen once before, when Pickles the dog uncovered it in south London beneath a hedge in the run-up to the 1966 World Cup, and survived the second world war when Ottorino Barassi, president of the champion Italian Football Federation, hid it in a shoe-box under his bed to prevent it falling into the hands of the Nazis). The Eastman Kodak Company would later donate a copy of the cup to Brazil.

Another reason for its reluctance is the simple cost. The current 6.175kg Fifa World Cup Trophy – 5kg of 18 carat goal and two layers of malachite – cost $50,000 to make back in 1970 and is worth millions today. When it was made, the Italian sculptor Silvio Gazzaniga described his creation in the following grandiose terms: "The lines spring out from the base, rising in spirals, stretching out to receive the world. From the remarkable dynamic tensions of the compact body of the sculpture rise the figures of two athletes at the stirring moment of victory." It might sound pretentious to you and me, but Fifa clearly agrees that the trophy is something special too – which is why its regulations state that the trophy will not be changing owners.

"I reckon that Steve Bruce once scored 20-plus goals in a season for Manchester United. Is this correct or am a I dreaming?"

Bruce came ever so close to reaching this mark, but he did not quite manage 20 goals. He did get within a whisker though during a remarkable 1990-91 season, when he put 19 into the back of the net (11 of which were penalties). As Bruce related in FourFourTwo magazine: "Obviously 19 goals is something I am quite proud of ... but one thing that does irk from that season is that I scored against Barcelona in the Cup Winners' Cup final, but Mark Hughes nicked it, otherwise I would have hit the magical 20 mark, and that was a big disappointment." Bruce never came close to breaking the 20-goal barrier again and although he earned a reputation for being a goalscoring centre-half, it was largely based on that one season: in 414 appearances for Manchester United between 1987 and 1996, he only scored 52 goals.

"Are there are any famous footballers who smoked cigarettes regularly?"

Far more than you may care to imagine and far more to list comprehensively here. Most recently, the Manchester United forward Dimitar Berbatov was snapped with a fag languidly hanging out of the side of his mouth, defending himself in the Independent by saying: "Sometimes when you see a picture, I pretend to smoke to make me more of a cool guy." Hmm. At least the Portsmouth and England goalkeeper David James had the good grace to own up to his craving, revealing in 2008 that he'd had a 20-a-day habit for the past 15 years. "I spent most of my career puffing away on fags: after training, before matches and even on the team coach," he wrote in the Observer. "It makes me ill just thinking about it."

James pointed to Zinedine Zidane, who was also got by photographers taking a crafty drag in the run-up to France's 2006 World Cup semi-final against Portugal. Around that time, the Guardian reported that "an aged but reputable study of 1,559 English professional footballers showed that cigarette smoking was much lower than the national average – only 5% admitted to it", but it also noted the 1998 pro-smoking group Forest's all-smoking fantasy team, comprising Dino Zoff, Socrates, Gerson, Jack Charlton, Frank Leboeuf, Jimmy Greaves, David Ginola, Osvaldo Ardiles, Malcolm McDonald, Bobby Charlton and Robert Prosinecki, with Paul Gascoigne on the bench.

Gascoigne had been unmasked as a serial puffer prior to

the 1998 World Cup. However, Glenn Hoddle, the England manager at the time, decided to take a very softly, softly approach. "Paul's been smoking since he was in Rome with Lazio, six or seven years," he said. "If I tried to stop him for three weeks now, it might have an adverse effect. Ossie Ardiles was on 40-a-day when he won the World Cup with Argentina, and there's a fellow called Gianluca Vialli at Chelsea too," Hoddle added, warming to his theme. "It didn't bother Ossie and it doesn't bother me." Of course, only a few months later, Hoddle famously kicked a tearful Gazza out of his World Cup squad and the rest has been a sad history.

Nowadays, there is often shock if Wayne Rooney and William Gallas are papped in the company of Nasty Nicotine (which they both have), but football's association with cigarettes used to be far greater, and much more visible. Cigarette companies openly sought out footballers with their collectable cards, while players were more than happy to endorse the products they so often partook in. Dixie Dean promoted Carreras Clubs – "the cigarettes with a kick in them" – back in the 1930s, the non-smoking Stanley Matthews happily attributed his "smooth ball control" to the "smoothness of Craven A", while the former Manchester United player Charlie Roberts set up a tobacconist business after his playing days, even developing a cigar called Ducrobel, so named after the United trio Dick Duckworth, Charlie Roberts and Alex Bell.

In Jackie Milburn's autobiography, he recalled the final moments before Newcastle United's 1951 FA Cup final against Blackpool, rushing to the toilets for a sneaky smoke, only to find four of his team-mates there already doing likewise. "No fewer than nine of our team smoked and on three occasions at Wembley in a Cup final, I've sat at half-time having a fag," he wrote. Milburn scored twice in Newcastle's 2-0 win that day but would later die of lung cancer. Johan Cruyff was another heavy smoker throughout his career and only gave up after undergoing double heart bypass surgery in 1991 (he would later front a Catalan health department campaign, declaring: "Football has given me everything in life. Smoking nearly took it all away").

As for the smoking supremo, it is hard to look beyond the aforementioned Socrates, who captained Brazil in two ultimately unsuccessful World Cups and got through at least one pack a day, sometimes two. When, more than a decade after retiring, he made one of the most implausible comebacks in history, for Garforth Town of the Northern Counties East League Division One, the qualified doctor managed no more than a 12-minute cameo. "It was far too cold. The second I got out I had this incredible headache," he declared afterwards. Then again, as the Brazilian had explained in the run-up to the game, his expectations were not particularly high: "I smoke 20 cigarettes a day and I have a beer now and then. I can't kick the cigarettes, but what can you do?"

"I remember reading that when the Premiership began, there were only nine foreigners (not UK and Ireland players) that started for the clubs. Is this true? And if so, who were they?"

Close, but no cigar. The actual number in their teams' starting line-ups when the league kicked off in August 1992 was 10 – with two more coming on as substitutes. The 10 were: John Jensen (Arsenal), Anders Limpar (Arsenal), Eric Cantona (Leeds United), Michel Vonk (Manchester City), Peter Schmeichel (Manchester United), Andrei Kanchelskis (Manchester United), Gunner Halle (Oldham Athletic), Jan Stejskal (QPR), Roland Nilsson (Sheffield Wednesday) and Hans Segers (Wimbledon). Robert Warzycha (Everton) came on as a replacement that weekend, as did Liverpool's Ronnie Rosenthal. Compare and contrast with the random sample from the Premier League fixtures of 20-21 March 2010, when 109 of the starting 220 players were foreign.

"Who was the first player to miss a penalty in a shoot-out during a British football match?"

Cast your mind back to the summer of 1970, if you will. Elvis was enjoying a six-week stay at No. 1 with the Wonder of You, Carlos Alberto was basking in the glory of lifting the Jules Rimet Trophy for Brazil, and a beaming Ted Heath had just become British prime minister.

Meanwhile, on 1 August, a full-strength Manchester United team found themselves in Hull, playing in the semi-final of the Watney Mann Invitation Cup.

What, you might ask? And we were inclined to do the same. Bizarrely, it was a Cup tournament restricted to the two highest scoring teams from each division, excluding those recently promoted, relegated or in Europe. United made it in by scoring 66 goals as they finished eighth in the First Division; Hull because they had topped the Second Division scoring charts with 72 goals. More peculiarly still, the FA had decided to allow – for the first time – penalty shoot-outs to be used if the matches were tied.

Guess what happened next? That's right – both Hull and United made it through their quarter-finals (against Reading and Peterborough, respectively) and, when their match finished 1-1 after extra-time, the scene was set for Britain's first penalty shoot-out. George Best took the first spot-kick, scoring low to the keeper's right. The next five penalties were also dispatched with ease, before Denis Law stepped up and saw his kick saved by Ian McKechnie, thus becoming the first player to ever miss in a shoot-out. Not that it mattered much: Hull missed their next two penalties (the decisive one from McKechnie) and United edged through to the final (where they lost 4-1 at Derby).

You know the rest. That year, the shoot-out was adopted by Uefa and Fifa, and before long England and missed penalties were going together as nicely as butter on hot toast. As for the Watney Cup, it lasted three more years (won by Colchester United, Bristol Rovers and Stoke City) before going the way of the Soccer Six, Mitropa Cup and the Cup Winners' Cup.

"Can you explain to me how Djibril Cissé became the Lord of the Manor of Frodsham?"

After buying a £2m house with nine acres of land in the village of Frodsham, Cheshire, overlooking the Mersey in May 2005, the then Liverpool striker inherited the title to boot. Traceable back to the Domesday Book in 1086 and once used by Edward the Black Prince in the 14th century, the title gave Cissé the right to allow fox hunting on his property. Which he swiftly refused, thus infuriating the local Cheshire Forest Hunt. "These titles signify nothing," Charles Mosley of Debrett's Peerage told the Independent. "They should not be confused with the titles of honour – a mistake many people make. Hitherto, it has not been something footballers have gone after, but they are millionaires now and a title is something to add to their possessions."

"With Portsmouth having gone into administration, with perhaps even worse down the line to come, I was wondering which club was the most successful that now doesn't exist?"

Football's not such a funny old game any more. We've largely had the same set of clubs hanging around at the top end of the game for years, but Manchester United fans should not feel too blasé: a quick rifle through the well-thumbed annals of history suggests that quite a number of national champions have not so much failed to last the test of time, as completely flunked it.

Belfast Celtic won 19 Irish titles and eight cups before withdrawing from the league in 1949. In Scotland, Third Lanark, title winners in 1904, cup winners in 1889 and 1905, and finalists on a further four occasions – the most recent in 1938 – went to the wall in 1967. Many Thirds fans were lost to the game, though many went on to support a team based barely a mile from Thirds' Cathkin Park, the Scottish Junior League side Pollok who, to this day, regularly pull attendances greater than some in the Scottish Second and Third Divisions.

The New York Cosmos franchise won five North American Soccer League titles during their 14 years of existence between 1971 and 1985, before going belly up along with the rest of the NASL. In Belgium, RWD Molenbreek (1974-75 league champions) were forced to dissolve in 2002, while in Germany, Karlsruher FV (1910 champions) and VfB Leipzig (1903, 1906 and 1913) have both gone bust in the past 20 years. As with Third Lanark (now playing in the Greater Glasgow Amateur League), "phoenix" sides were subsequently created in each case except for the Cosmos, but have yet to achieve the glories of their originals. Most recently, the Dutch club HFC Haarlem, 1946 national champions, went bankrupt in January 2010, former player Ruud Gullit telling De Telefgraaf: "Let's be honest, nobody came to watch any more. So you have to ask yourself what the rationale of their existence was. You can't live off your past and your memories."

"Has a club ever won a European trophy and been relegated in the same season? If not, who has come the closest?"

You would like to think that in 54 years of European club competition that there would be at least one example of this dastardly double. Alas, for pub-quiz setters everywhere, no such instance exists. But one team came mighty close: the Internazionale side of 1993-94.

That season, they shaded the likes of Norwich City, Borussia Dortmund and Cagliari to reach the Uefa Cup final, where they overcame Salzburg 2-0 on aggregate. However, in Serie A they wheezed like an obese man on a treadmill, despite boasting the likes of Dennis Bergkamp, Walter Zenga, Wim Jonk and Nicola Berti in their side, and eventually finished 13th – just one point and two places ahead of relegated Piacenza.

"Francesco Totti, famously, can never leave Roma since his mother threatened to cut off 'whatever' if he did. Are there similar examples of forced allegiance in football?"

Well, there was David Unsworth, who asked to leave West Ham in the summer of 1998. Aston Villa and Unsworth's first club Everton both made bids but, despite his family home being on Merseyside, he chose Villa. After just one week, however, Unsworth was apparently "advised" by wife Jane to tell the Villa manager John Gregory that he had made a mistake and that he should have rejoined the Toffees. Unsworth cited a lengthy commute as the reason for his change of heart but Gregory, not known for his moderate man management, wasn't buying it and sent his new signing back to Merseyside to "sort his head out". Unsworth promptly signed for Everton, Villa recouping the same £3m fee they had paid West Ham just a few weeks earlier. "You know what players are like," seethed Gregory. "He probably thought Birmingham was just outside Bolton. After his first day at the club it took him three hours to get home and when he did, his meal was in the cat or the bin. There was his wife Jane to deal with – she obviously wears the trousers in their household. It could be Girl Power, call it what you like."

The former Sunderland manager Roy Keane wasn't a fan of footballers' other halves either. In August 2007, after a series of failed attempts to persuade players to move to the north-east, Keane railed: "I find it a bit of a surprise ... that players let their wives decide. I think it is weak. Weak." He went on to add: "If someone doesn't want to come to Sunderland then all well and good. But if they don't want to come to Sunderland because their wife wants to go shopping in London, then it is a sad state of affairs. This side of it, with the women running the show, concerns and worries me."

Samuel Eto'o came within a whisker of joining Chelsea in 2005, but admitted that his significant other was reluctant to give up their life in Barcelona for a move to England. "[She] put her foot down over the idea of packing our bags and going to a city like London and I have to respect her," he told the Mirror. "I had an offer from Chelsea, but I was always clear I wanted to stay at Barça." In 2009 he, wife Georgette and their children moved to Milan, where he had signed for Inter.

"In which year did Bradford Park Avenue leave the Football League?"

Not many football fans under 30 would have heard of Bradford Park Avenue: like Small Heath, Darwen and other clubs that left the Football League some time ago, they seem to have been quietly forgotten. But BPA deserve better than that. During their 62-year stay in the league, they graced the First Division, reached three FA Cup quarter-finals, and held the registration of one of British football's great players: Len Shackleton.

Vice-president of the club before his death in November 2000, Shackleton scored a record 171 goals in six years from 1940-46. Although the club's fortunes dipped in the 1950s, BPA were clearly planning for a brighter future when their new floodlights were officially opened by the Czechoslovakia World Cup side in October 1961. Instead the skies darkened. During the latter half of the 1960s, the club's fortunes began to slide and, in 1970, following three successive last-place finishes in the Football League, they were replaced by Cambridge United of the Southern League.

The situation soon went from dark to desperate. By 1974 the club had been liquidated with debts of £57,652, but the supporters refused to give up. They registered the name as a company and began again in the Bradford Amateur Sunday League Division Four, playing in the old kit of the former club, until the "old" club was reformed in 1987. BPA are still going strong and, at the time of writing, have risen to the top of the UniBond Premier Division.

"Who was the first manager to win the European Cup with two different clubs?"

The man you are looking for is Austrian Ernst Happel. He coached Feyenoord to a 2-1 victory over Celtic in 1970 and, 13 years later, guided SV Hamburg to a 1-0 success in the final against Juventus. Happel's achievements don't end there: he also coached Club Brugge in their

European Cup defeat to Liverpool in 1978 and, in the same year, led Holland to the final of the 1978 World Cup. He died in 1992, but his memory lives on. The Austrian national stadium – the Ernst Happel Stadion – is named in his honour.

"I recently watched a re-run of the 1974 World Cup final between Holland and West Germany. Both teams were kitted out by adidas (they of the three stripes), but Johan Cruyff's shirt had only two stripes on the sleeve. Any idea how come?"

The story goes a little something like this. The Dutch FA had a deal with adidas to supply its stripy orange kit, which your Johnny Reps and Rob Rensenbrinks of this world were only too happy to wear during the finals in Germany. Cruyff, of course, had other ideas. He had an exclusive personal deal with adidas's rivals Puma, who supplied him with their classic Puma King boots. Because of this, he was unwilling to sport the three trademark stripes of adidas and insisted on a special two-striped version instead. As you would expect, he got exactly what he wanted.

Although Cruyff wasn't around to cause the German kit giants bother when Holland embarked on their 1978 World Cup campaign, his rebellious spirit lived on. The Van de Kerkhof twins, Rene and Willy, insisted on being issued with Cruyff-style two-striped shirts, or else they were off. But did the Dutch FA capitulate in the face of this blatant show of player power? Of course it did.

"Post-match player interviews are usually desperately bland. Are there any that have been livened up with a footballer swearing live on TV?"

Micah Richards needed only four first-team appearances with Manchester City to enter this particular hall of fame. Having scored a last-minute equaliser at Aston Villa to take their FA Cup fifth-round tie to a replay in May 2006, Richards was thus interviewed by Garth Crooks live on BBC1. "Well Micah, an extraordinary finish. What did you make of it?" went Crooks's probing line of questioning. "Oh, it was just great to be out there … fuck yeah, you know … I just can't believe it," went the reply. A stunned Crooks quickly found his feet to say: "Well, you're a young lad and we can understand your excitement, but this is going out to a national audience, so be careful what you say."

Managers aren't much better, even when they're as experienced as Sir Alex Ferguson, who gave Sky's Geoff Shreeves short shrift after the November 2005 win over Chelsea, when he asked if the Manchester United manager had "known more pressure on you or more questions about you in your 19-year tenure here?" A red rag to a bullish Ferguson. "No, that's absolute bollocks that, absolute nonsense," he declared. "There's always pressure here … you know we went 13 games without winning once? People forget these things." After several seconds, Shreeves manages to stammer out: "I'll have to ask you to mind your language, there are children watching." Ferguson and Shreeves would have another run-in (sadly never broadcast) after the reporter asked Cristiano Ronaldo about his role in a dubious penalty decision at Middlesbrough in 2007 (save to say, it involved a liberal sprinkling of the words eff and cee), but since then, during their regular chinwags, the pair have appeared more than amicable towards each other.

That's pretty much that regarding post-match chit-chat, but it would be remiss of us to ignore Sky's infamous Goals on Sunday episode, involving the Derby County goalkeeper Stephen Bywater in 2007. Discussing his time at West Ham while working under the late Les Sealey, with co-hosts Claire Tomlinson and Chris Kamara, Tomlinson asks about the player's shirt number. "Do you still wear it now, No. 43, at Derby?" she queries. Bywater replies: "Yeah, I still wear it for as long as I keep playing because I know he'll be watching and he'll want me to do well. He'll always say: 'Don't be a ... don't be a ... [pauses, before very deliberately spelling out] C-U-N-T to yourself and just be a professional, be a man and do things right. Just be the best.' And I'll always remember that."

Kamara was also on the Goals on Sunday sofa when Roberto di Matteo said "you can't be tactically ... shit to be successful in Europe". His co-presenter on this occasion, Rob McCaffrey, responded by smirking: "That's a word that Dennis Wise taught him all those years ago

and it's not Roberto's fault with that, it's Dennis's fault."
And while we won't go into Joe Kinnear's infamous first
expletive-laden press conference as Newcastle manager
(in which he swore an impressive 46 times), he does make
this list for an exchange with Football Focus host Manish
Bhasin: "He's [Mike Ashley] the one who's cleared the
debts; he's the one who's put the money in. He's the one
who's got Newcastle out of the shit." Not exactly suitable
for Saturday lunchtime viewing, we're sure you'll agree.

Acknowledgements

As was the case in the first edition of The Knowledge, the list of contributors and colleagues who have tirelessly given their time and help to the column over the past decade is a lengthy one. Again, my apologies to anyone who has been unfairly forgotten. John Ashdown, Sean Ingle, Scott Murray and Rob Smyth deserve particular thanks for their hard work and footballing brains, as well as Georgina Turner, Paul Doyle, Tom Lutz, Paolo Bandini, Mike Adamson, Sid Lowe, Raphael Honigstein, Jonathan Wilson and Barry Glendenning, plus many, many others, including the good people behind the sterling website rsssf.com. Helen Brooks and Lisa Darnell from Guardian Books, and Sophie Lazar from Random House, have kindly helped make this book a reality, and for that I must thank them too. Last, but most definitely not least, Knowledge readers deserve special appreciation. Without their questioning minds, investigative assistance and yearning for seemingly mindless trivia, the column would not be what it is today. For that, again, thank you.